The Glory of Opera

The Glory of Opera

Alan Jefferson

Exeter Books

NEW YORK

Copyright © 1976 by Webb & Bower Ltd

Published in USA 1983
by Exeter Books
Distributed by Bookthrift
Exeter is a trademark of Simon & Schuster, Inc.
Bookthrift is a registered trademark of Simon & Schuster, Inc.
New York, New York

ISBN 0-671-06142-9

Printed in Singapore

Contents

For Adam

Opera is the greatest and most glorious artistic phenomenon which our civilisation possesses. It is a fusion of music, art and drama. Music alone can interest us, and it can produce different sensations and meanings for each listener: its acceptance is very personal. Pure art – painting, sculpture, cartoons – speaks with a silent voice. Sometimes we can feel what it is saying, sometimes it is beyond us. Actors at the play state their intentions clearly but we have to be in tune with their idiom. At the opera we are drawn into a story. The singers enact it for us in their special convention which we must accept. The music not only supports them as they talk or soliloquise but sometimes tells us things that they don't know or can't yet understand. This draws us in even closer until we are part of the drama, because opera demands that we give too. And by giving, we get back so much.

Alan Jefferson

I Poetry, Prose and Patter

The Beggar's Opera (Gay-Pepusch, Lincoln's Inn Fields) seen in a painting by William Hogarth and showing Lucy Lockett appealing for the life of the highwayman hero, Macheath, in prison

The argument: Words or Music first? will always resound so long as there is an operatic form as we know it. Each of the two protagonists, poet and composer, will state and support his own case, except the few whose knowledge of their art is deep and generous enough to make it a joint affair, a pure welding of words and music, neither being superior to nor independent of the other any longer. If this state of affairs comes to pass, we have a masterpiece.

It is easy enough to find examples of the composer who is far more powerful than the librettist – in reputation, in experience and in authority. Then he will bully his partner to the extent of commanding: 'Put some words to this next section that I've composed, and let me have it back. I'll tell you if I approve them and I'll alter them if I don't.' This is no way for a good opera to proceed in any sense, least of all in co-ordination of thought and effort. Neither does the reverse work when the poet says: 'Here's my text for the whole work, and it's a gem, a real work of art. I've done it all myself and you just dare to alter a single word!'

Although, of the very early operas, more librettos exist than scores, the words themselves mean very little in this form. They are a long way from being any more than mild gibberish. For a long time, few of the composers and librettists really bothered to put their heads together. In George Frederick Handel's time opera was at the mercy of the castrati who decided what they would sing and then proceeded to change it by elaborate, often spontaneous variation, in which no words could mean anything.

But before Handel had given up opera in London as a bad job, John Gay and Dr Pepusch compiled (rather than created) *The Beggar's Opera* (1728) with its cast of rogues and thieves and a highwayman for a hero. It used Gay's sparkling dialogue and either folk-songs or tunes from other composers' works. Thus Handel found some of his best-known arias being filched and used out of context to vulgar words in this and in the flood of ballad operas which followed. But *The Beggar's Opera* is important for being the first of its kind, for dealing with some of the dregs of humanity, and for possessing a universal story. It reached New York in 1750 where its additional surprises, such as mocking at English politicians, and the warring opera singers, were enjoyed in America. John Gay's name shines brightly among librettists, for he was a real originator.

The librettist is the man who gives the singers words to sing. Whether they can make them heard, whether they even understand them, is sometimes another matter. Were there no words at all, merely *melismata* – ooh'd and aah'd sounds – beautifully sung, it would surely be difficult to maintain any interest; but as soon as somebody on the stage utters the word 'No!' – and in very nearly every Western language it sounds much the same – we have a situation. A good story is built up of situations: they have to exist, there has to be controversy or even something more aggressive.

Even so, a good opera libretto is not one consisting of a lot of people all saying 'No!' to one another; neither is it an easy piece of work which anybody can knock up in five minutes. It needs refinement in the telling of the story, even if its characters are thieves and villains (then even more so); in the use of words to create perspective in their own presence; in the awareness of what vowels cannot be sung at the top, or bottom, of the voice; in the delineation of characters with strength and economy. And a lot more besides. When Christopher Hassall and Sir William Walton were writing their opera *Troilus and Cressida*, Hassall was in London and Walton was in Italy. For much of the time they corresponded and used the libretto of Giuseppe Verdi's *Rigoletto* to give patterns of words and balance between set-piece arias or ensembles. There cannot very well be three long arias in succession and then four choruses – to give an

9

Above: Un Ballo in Maschera
(Verdi–Somma/Scribe). The finale
of the opera in a production at
Sadler's Wells in 1966. Renato has
assassinated Riccardo from
mainly jealous and partly political
reasons after suspecting him with
his wife Amelia. Amelia is cleared
of adultery but faces a doubtfully
happy life in exile with Renato

Opposite: Troilus and Cressida
(Walton–Hassall, Covent Garden,
1954). In this scene from the
opera's world première, Richard
Lewis as Troilus and Magda
László as Cressida are seen at the
height of their love which is soon
to bring them to disaster

absurd example. A look at any libretto will show a mixture of verse: long lines, short lines, then perhaps a chunk of prose, then a concerted number (duet, trio, quartet and so on) and back to an aria with pithy phrasing. Not that there is the least resemblance between *Troilus and Cressida* and *Rigoletto*, or that the Verdi opera in any way influenced Walton. In fact Hassall had never heard *Rigoletto* and was horrified after he had done so, for he found its medieval cruelty painful to the Greek mood he was in and was trying to extend into everyday twentieth-century comprehension. Still, it served its purpose, to produce verbal shapes and patterns on the page, and as a working template.

The first librettist of international status was Pietro Armando Dominico Trapassi, usually known as Metastasio. He was appointed Court Poet at Vienna at the age of thirty-one in 1729, and wrote some fifty librettos which were used over and over again to the total of one thousand times. For instance, Mozart's *La Clemenza di Tito* was to a Metastasio text and Gluck also used it. There is fair proof that no other libretto has been reset more times than this story.

The law of copyright is a recent institution and does not even yet secure recognition and payment to the owner throughout the world. In Metastasio's day there was no such thing, and a libretto which had been the basis for a successful opera was fair game to all and sundry who might wish to cash in on a success today in the hope of creating an even bigger one tomorrow. Daniel Auber's opera *Gustavus III* used a libretto adapted from Eugène Scribe's play, which Verdi took over word for word, forcing Auber's work into oblivion. Verdi's opera was called *Un Ballo in Maschera* ('A Masked Ball').

Eugène Scribe (1791–1861) was even more prolific than Metastasio and lived in an age when opera had changed its direction. But both Scribe and Meta-

Arrigo Boito (1842–1918). A poet and a trained musician. He wrote the libretto for Amilcare Ponchielli's La Gioconda *and then created* Otello *and* Falstaff *for Verdi to set. His own operas are* Mefistofele *and* Nerone. *A very talented man who provided Verdi, at the end of his career, with his two best libretti*

stasio had one thing in common: they knew how to give the public what it wanted. Metastasio excelled in delightful and fluent verse in a classical atmosphere where complicated plots and declamations were carried on between royalty (or, at a pinch, the aristocracy) and the gods. There were no common people. So far so good, for his age. But Scribe had a different public to please and they wanted thoroughly skilful plots constructed economically but in less flowery, simpler language. The character-building did not concern them. What Scribe possessed was an intuitive flair for theatrical effects, what the French so succinctly call *coups de théâtre*. They were indeed blows, and they went home as never before. One has only to think of a handful of his librettos: *La Sonnambula, L'Elisir d'Amore, Les Huguenots, Le Comte Ory*, to appreciate what good theatre they are. The 'Scribe Factory', as his study was called, ultimately consisted of seventy-six volumes of his complete works, and they included ninety-seven opera librettos.

Since then no one librettist, let alone a poet, has been so prolific – and we must take care not to imagine that every librettist *was* a poet. Ideally he can be, for a poet should be a master of words, able to make them work overtime in setting a scene or explaining something about a person. If Mozart can be described as the most *poetic* composer, it might be on account of Lorenzo Da Ponte, his librettist for *Figaro, Don Giovanni* and *Così fan Tutte.*

Da Ponte was a truly remarkable man. He was born in 1749 into a very poor family, took the name of his benefactor, a bishop, and received no education until he was fourteen. After only five years of concentrated study he went to Venice but became involved in romantic scandals that obliged him to leave. He eventually found himself in Vienna where he exercised sufficient charm and ability to be recommended to the Emperor and to fill the post of Court Poet recently vacated by Metastasio's death. Here he became a close friend of Mozart and between 1786 and 1789 he wrote the three matchless librettos. A month after the première of *Così fan Tutte* the Emperor died and Da Ponte left Vienna for London. Despite becoming a teacher of Italian and poet to the Italian Opera there, his debts were beginning to overtake him. Always accustomed to luxuries, he was now on the downward slope of his life. London could not afford him and so he went to America, gradually failing in tea and tobacco enterprises. The inevitable Italian teaching did not help to establish him either, and he had almost lost all connection with the opera when the Garcia family arrived to give the New York premières of a number of operas. Although he had never met Garcia, Da Ponte called on him and said 'I am Da Ponte, author of the libretto of *Don Giovanni* and a friend of Mozart'. Garcia was so overcome that he embraced the poet and sang Don Giovanni's 'Champagne Aria'. But poor Da Ponte died in 1838 in his ninetieth year, sad and forgotten.

Successive composers have looked to the divine Mozart for inspiration and guidance, and most of them have realised the part that Da Ponte played in causing Mozart's own inspiration to flow so freely.

Verdi suffered many hardships with his early librettos but ended his composing life with an exceptional librettist: Arrigo Boito. These associations are all documented and offer fascinating reading; and so does the career of another man, Richard Wagner. He was indeed many-headed in his variety of capacities: opera composer, musician, poet, political wrangler, exile and rebel, man of the theatre, expert on a wide range of subjects from new musical instruments and their construction to fund-raising (for himself), and seduction of other men's wives. He had no difficulties with his librettist who always produced exactly what was needed to be set to music, for the simple reason that he always wrote his own texts. His diaries and notebooks tell of all his accomplishments in detail.

Richard Wagner (1813–83). The
great German innovator of the
Gesamtkunstwerk ; revolutionary;
womaniser ; composer–conductor–
librettist. He had many failures
and disappointments but refused
to be put off, and his ultimate
success and achievements
certainly demand that he be
called a genius

Wagner's method of writing his largest operatic work was somewhat unusual. He had taken the hero Siegfried from Norse legends and wrote a libretto
which he called 'Siegfried's Death'. In so doing he discovered enough new
material for a second opera and wrote the book for 'The Young Siegfried'. But
this needed so much explanation that, again going backwards in the course of
the great legend, Wagner was obliged to write 'The Valkyrie' that told of Siegfried's parents (brother and sister) and how they were only tools of a higher
power. Again this needed amplifying, and although Wagner now had three full-
length, three-act opera librettos it was necessary to preface them by another,
different in construction, to emphasise its place and its subordinate purpose.

Hence the gods were shown coming in first, and going out last, giving an excellent shape to the whole tetralogy and making the story fully comprehensible. Thus 'The Rhinegold' comes first, *Die Walküre* second, plain *Siegfried* third, and *Götterdämmerung* or 'The Twilight of the Gods' describes this as well as Siegfried's death, for they are related. It all grew backwards but had to be composed forwards, for Wagner's use of recurrent themes or *Leitmotive* are the ever-flowering result of his characters' actions, thoughts, motives throughout the whole great span of nearly twenty hours. In each of the operas after the first one in *Der Ring des Nibelungen*, as the cycle is called, there is a great recapitulatory scene by one of the characters which can be seen as Wagner's method of filling in what was eventually to become the stuff of the preceding opera in the story. And he left it in as a kind of *aide-mémoire* for the audience.

Wagner's librettos are worth looking at in their original German just for the shape of the lines upon the page. He made great use of a short and urgent metre called *Stabreim* which means an alliterative rhyme. The dwarf Mime in *Siegfried*, terrified by the thought of a dragon which inhabits a nearby cave, sings:

> *Was flackert und lackert,*
> *was flimmert und schwirrt,*
> *was schwebt dort und webt,*
> *und wabert umher?*
> *Dort glimmert's und glitzt's in der Sonne Gluth!*

Even to one who knows no German, these words need little explanation in their onomatopoeia.

In *Tristan und Isolde*, one of the world's greatest love stories, Wagner (who understood such situations intimately from personal experience) gave the two lovers an ecstatic greeting. This comes in the second act after they have drunk a love potion but have never been alone together since:

> Tristan: *Isolde! Geliebte!*
> Isolde: *Tristan! Geliebter! Bist du mein?*
> Tristan: *Hab' ich dich wieder?*
> Isolde: *Darf ich dich fassen?*
> Tristan: *Kann ich mir trauen?*
> Isolde: *Endlich! Endlich!*
> Tristan: *An meiner Brust!* . . . and so on

It is carried through at great speed and with extreme ecstasy in such a manner as to earn it the nickname of the 'telegram duet'.

Wagner's librettos are not great poetry, but as intensely imaginative works of verbal imagery they make marvellous texts for music, especially when they are put together with such skill and understanding of this, their ultimate requirement. Even so, Wagner insisted upon giving readings of his music dramas to his disciples before he had written a note of the scores which ultimately clothed them, skin-tight, so that nobody today would ever consider separating the words and hearing them aloud. On the other hand, the music is sometimes played without the words, but it takes on a very diluted effect.

One libretto comes to mind as being so finely wrought that it can stand alone and has been performed as a most successful reading. This is Hugo von Hofmannsthal's text for *Der Rosenkavalier*, to music by Richard Strauss. Strauss inherited Richard Wagner's mantle, though to emphasise how far below his illustrious musical forbear he felt himself to be, Strauss declared: 'There is no Richard II!' His partnership with Hofmannsthal began in 1906 and had immediate fruition in *Elektra*, the poet's 'new' treatment of the old Greek legend as told by Sophocles, with distinctly advanced psychological overtones. Hofmannsthal was an Austrian with Italian and Jewish blood, who lived on the outskirts of Vienna for most of his life and wrote highly charged poetic plays besides six librettos for Strauss. He was opposed to naturalism in the theatre, and almost everything he wrote was skilfully balanced by opposites as if to

METROPOLITAN OPERA HOUSE

SEASON OF 1886-87

EDMUND C. STANTON, DIRECTOR OF THE OPERA

Wednesday Evening, Dec. 1, 1886,

Tristan and Isolde.

MUSIC-DRAMA IN THREE ACTS.

BY RICHARD WAGNER.

ITS FIRST PRODUCTION IN AMERICA.

KNABE PIANOS: used.

NIGHTLY PRICES OF ADMISSION.

ORCHESTRA CHAIRS	$4.00
DRESS CIRCLE CHAIRS	2.50
BALCONY, FRONT ROWS	1.50
" OTHER ROWS	1.00
FAMILY CIRCLE	.50
BAGNOIR BOXES (6 Seats)	30.00
FIRST TIER BOXES (6 Seats)	60.00

Doors open at 1:30 and 7:30 o'clock.

Performances commence at 2 and 8 precisely.

The Libretto sold in the house is the ONLY
authorized and correct Edition.

Opera Glasses to hire in the Lobby.

No fees to Box openers, and any inattention
should be reported to the Director's office.

accentuate the contradictions in his own life. He was self-tortured to a great extent, and in dealings with outsiders he was his own worst enemy. But his verse is magnificent, his imagination and finesse over his characters absolutely perfect, the patience to make them all three-dimensional is brilliantly effective. He was born in 1874 and died suddenly in 1929 of a stroke. Within the twenty-four years during which he worked with Strauss, they achieved nothing finer, more enduring or as fitting a tribute to Mozart as *Der Rosenkavalier* ('their *Figaro*', they called it, and indeed it bears many resemblances, without being derivative, both to *Die Meistersinger* and to *Figaro*).

What makes this particular partnership so interesting is the volume of correspondence from which we can follow the details of their progress with each opera. And since it is a book of *words*, it is very informative over the actual difficulties that the poet encountered in the course of each creation. It was some time, for instance, before he told Strauss how disappointed he had been with the way in which the words for the Lackeys at the end of Act I of *Der Rosenkavalier* had been set. Hofmannsthal is clearly the more temperamental, the more easily offended, the more uncertain of the two men, always ready to justify what he has done but still handing out this handsome bouquet to Strauss's wife: 'In the joint work we have done in the past or may do in the future, I consider Dr Strauss entirely as the principal partner and the music as the dominant one among the elements joined together.'

Strauss's subsequent librettists did not approach Hofmannsthal: Stefan Zweig was politically undesirable in the new Germany of the 1930s and was forced to leave; Joseph Gregor was a dry-as-dust scholar whose three librettos for Strauss were accepted *faute-de-mieux*. Only the last opera, *Capriccio*, which was a joint effort between Strauss and the conductors Clemens Krauss and Hans Swarowsky, came near to being an artistic whole.

The next librettists of merit were Anglo-Saxon. Montagu Slater's text for *Peter Grimes* helped to establish Benjamin Britten as England's white hope of opera after the last war. Since then Britten has composed more than fifteen stage works (and one television opera) although none has been superior to the first. *Gloriana*, which was commissioned for the Coronation Season in London in 1953, had a text by William Plomer after Lytton Strachey that showed an unflattering aspect of Queen Elizabeth I that greatly displeased Her Majesty Queen Elizabeth II.

Britten's *Midsummer Night's Dream* has a libretto by himself and his principal tenor, Peter Pears, after Shakespeare. This is an interesting progression from Wagner's day when one of the voices to be heard in the opera adds his knowledge to the choice of text. This has not happened since Schikanaeder was Papageno in *Die Zauberflöte*.

Most of Shakespeare's plays are stage-proof but it does not necessarily follow that any of the plays will succeed when transformed into an opera. Something of its original state will have been removed, and purists of literature (among them Richard Strauss) have deplored such burglary at the expense of the poet's inspiration and craft. Strauss would never conduct Verdi's *Otello* out of respect for Shakespeare; nor *Don Carlos* or *Guillaume Tell* (Schiller), nor *Faust* especially, for it was Goethe's masterpiece as he left it.

Stravinsky's last opera, *The Rake's Progress*, has a spry and very singable libretto by W. H. Auden and Chester Kallman, based on Hogarth's pictures, and carried through partly as a pastiche, in words and in music. The same authors created *Elegy for Young Lovers* for Hans Werne Henze ten years after. As Auden is a poet in his own right, there is inspirational fire in both these librettos.

The translation of opera librettos is a subject all of its own, and sometimes the result is far removed from the original libretto in sense, atmosphere and

Opposite (inset): Hugo von Hofmannsthal (1874–1929), remarkable Austrian poet and dramatist, best known in opera for his collaboration with Richard Strauss. This produced six operas of which Der Rosenkavalier *was financially most successful,* Die Frau ohne Schatten *the most imaginative and novel*

Richard Strauss (1864–1949), son of Munich's first horn-player and a brewery heiress, was writing for the voice at the age of 4½ and until he was 85. Two wars crippled him financially and after Hofmannsthal's death he suffered difficulties with librettists until his last opera Capriccio, *which he and Clemens Krauss wrote together*

Das Rheingold at Covent Garden in 1974. Donald McIntyre as Wotan, Ava June as Freia, Josephine Veasey as Fricka all wear 'anatomical' costumes and headgear which divorce the characters from any recognisable place or age

verbal colouring. Nowadays producers and singers are more particular as to what words are used, but it makes one wonder how our ancestors can have stomached this sort of thing:

'Wish-maid thou wert to me:
   against me thy wish has been turned;
Shield-maid thou wert to me:
   against me thy shield was up-raised;

Lot-chooser thou wert to me:
   against me the lot hast thou chosen;
Hero-stirrer thou wert to me:
   against me thou stirredst up heroes.'

'Hero-stirrer' forsooth! And how can one comfortably sing *stirredst*? This comes from Frederick Jameson's note-for-note translation of *Die Walküre*, this extract being part of Wotan's reproof to Brünnhilde in the last act. Mr Jameson was not the only mangler of English. A pair of translators of Wagner, the Corders, as well as a John Oxenford, all made merry havoc of Wagner's imposing German texts by turning them into barely comprehensible English.

In recent years there have been two complete reassessments of *Der Ring* in English, a singing version by Andrew Porter for the London Coliseum production, eminently sensible and faithful, and a reading version by William Mann that verges at times on the 'pop' and may be incomprehensible, in part, as soon as the expressions he uses have lost their currency. Both these gentlemen happen to be music critics.

It is but a short step to performances when totally unexpected words are uttered in the course of the opera. On one occasion an *Aida* was cast internationally: Aida, German; Radamès, Icelandic; Amonasro, Italian; King of Egypt, Polish; Amneris and Ramfis, English. Naturally the range of accents, all attempting English, would have fascinated Professor Higgins, though the

Aida insisted upon singing in German. At one point in the plot it is essential that the identity of one of the characters is made crystal clear to the audience, and here, with acute appreciation of dramatic needs, the soprano sang out confidentially to the front 'Gott! Mein Farder!'

In a provincial opera house in Germany, during a performance of *Ein Maskenball* by Verdi, the Samuel, perhaps exhausted and certainly confused, took a piece of paper given him in the course of the action. On it was written the name of the person who was to assassinate the King. With great delight he cried out 'Radamès!' (the hero of *Aida*). The possibilities open to them all in the next act make the mind boggle!

Such things can happen in a different language even when the text upon which the translation is based is a sensible and straightforward one. But the following doggerel may give a clue to the complications surrounding one of Verdi's operas:

> If you're not going far
> And you've got half an hour,
> I'll tell you the story
> Of *Il Trovatore.*

Most of the plot has already taken place long before the rise of the curtain, and this has to be related on the stage to some Spanish soldiers so that we, the audience, can be put in the picture. Admittedly this is the method used in the classic French drama, but it makes for tedium when adopted by a librettist, not only for the audience, but also for the Spanish soldiers.

Another Verdi opera, *La Forza del Destino*, has a plot of apparent coincidences heaped upon other unlikely happenings, after a young nobleman's pistol has accidentally gone off, killing his fiancée's father. People congregate in exactly the same inn in Spain after being separated; they meet again at exactly the same monastery somewhere else; and two ardent enemies become sworn friends because neither recognises the other abroad. But all this does not prevent *Forza* from being a wonderful opera.

Of all opera plots, *Euryanthe*, by Helmine von Chézy, is the most difficult to swallow, with the intervention of a spirit-woman, a dragon and a pair of villains who do their utmost to discredit a noblewoman's virtue. She assists them nobly by omitting to contradict them in public. In the end we are not quite sure what has happened, but Weber's score saves it from becoming a total failure. Helmine von Chézy, let it be said, is probably the only woman librettist of a significant opera.

Tragedies and vulgar comedies go well in German, farce sparkles in French, gloom and despondency belong to the Russians, while the Italians own so many operas of passion that they seldom need anybody else's, though their translations of German sound extra-terrestrial.

The question of 'language of the house' is altogether a vexed one, indeed it strikes one as being indefensible, when we consider with what pains the poet has constructed his libretto so that every word takes equal weight in the whole, consonants and vowels gaining maximum effect coupled with ease in diction and projection by the singers. The composer's work, which has followed, uses these same words and clothes them exactly in sounds. So to change them altogether into a different language seems inartistic. When that language can never provide identical depths of meaning for one or more words, and others have to be used with different connotations simply because they have the same number of syllables as the notes. . . .

Béla Bartók's opera *Bluebeard's Castle* has a text by Béla Balázs, in Hungarian of course. When this came to be translated into English, it was found that the Hungarian rhythm took on an uncomfortable similarity to 'Hiawatha', and it was as much as the translator could do to prevent the monotonous red-skin from interfering all the time.

The argument for 'language of the house' is that the audience can understand straight away what is happening on the stage. Since that presupposes excellent diction and a conductor who does not drown the singers, as well as clear production, the idiom may still be far from the familiar fireside. 'There is a truce with the Huns. Ezio, return at once to Rome' sounds remote, almost incomprehensible in English. What do a contemporary audience know of the Huns in any case? But put it back into Solera's comfortable Italian, and being at one stage removed from the start, we can far more easily accept:

Tregua è cogl' Unni.
A Roma, Ezio, tosto ritorna.

Operas whose librettos are initially in the language of the house are, of course a different matter, for then everything falls into place. But for English-

Below left: Giuseppe Verdi (1813–1901) the Italian opera composer of genius. In his own hand below the lithograph portrait is the 'Destiny' theme from his opera La Forza del Destino *in the ethereal form in which it is heard in the Monastery scene of Act II*

BEFORE THE CURTAIN

VERDI's appearance before the curtain on the production was the signal for an outburst of applause as has rarely been equalled, and when grasping the of the artists who had created the parts in his last bowed his acknowledgements to the brilliant a

THE PRODUCT

Below right: Verdi and the first-night cast of Falstaff, *caught by a lightning sketch in 1893 at La Scala, taking calls after the final curtain. Verdi was in his eightieth year*

speaking audiences and English operas it is a sad reflection that the language does not seem to have been devised for opera. Despite the large reservoir of its vocabulary, the subtlety and discretion available in choice of words, English never achieves when sung the imposing grandeur that it has when finely spoken. And when it is used in a translation from another language it invariably flattens and debases, even vulgarises, the original.

As long ago as the seventeenth century, only fifty years after the birth of opera, Purcell wrote these words which are the ideal for a librettist and composer to follow:

> Musick and Poetry have ever been acknowledged sisters, which, walking hand in hand, support each other; As Poetry is the harmony of words so Musick is that of notes; and as Poetry is a rise above Prose and Oratory, so is Musick the exaltation of Poetry. Both of them may excel apart, but surely they are most excellent when they are joyn'd, because nothing is then wanting to either of their proportions; for thus they appear like wit and beauty in the same person.

husiasm of the house knew no bounds. Of the Signor Maurel, who plays the title *rôle* of stands first, not only for his magnificent g of the music, but for the grace and ease with e wore a dress which, in a less accomplished artist, ave been made ridiculous. Signor Pino Corsi marked advance in his profession by his rendering

of the part of Ford, and the four Merry Wives, Signore Emma Zilli as Alice Ford, Adelina Stehle as Nannetta Ford, Virginia Guerrini as Meg, and Giuseppina Pasqua as Mrs. Quickly, won all hearts by the archness of their acting and the true spirit of comedy which they infused into the interpretation of their parts. The two tenors, Signori Garbin and Paroli, also did admir-

able service as Fenton and Dr. Caius, though, perhaps, the latter was not so well suited as he was in the part of Cassio in *Otello*. Signori Rossetti as Bardolpho and Arimondi as Pistola were also most excellent, and of Signor Mascheroni, the conductor, it can only be said, in the words which Verdi wrote across the portrait he presented to him, that he is "the brave commander of a brave army."

OI'S "FALSTAFF" AT MILÁN : SIGNOR VERDI APPEARING BEFORE THE CURTAIN WITH THE SINGERS

II
'Music, when soft voices die...'

Claudio Monteverdi (1567-1643). Italian opera composer who saw further into the possibilities of music for stage-works than any other before him had done. Many of his scores have been lost but those which survive mark him as a brilliant musician

Previous pages: Auditorium of Il Teatro alla Scala, Milan, taken from the prompt corner and showing the six tiers of seats and boxes which altogether hold 3,600 spectators. La Scala was opened in 1778, badly bombed in 1943, and reopened in May 1946

Opposite above: Beaux and ladies in the 'lobby' at the Drury Lane Theatre, London in the 1820s

Opposite below: A Rowlandson cartoon showing an untypically built castrato delivering a heroic aria

Overleaf: The Paris Opéra in the rue Lepeltier for a concert in 1829 to celebrate the birth of the Dauphin. Note the massive operatic scenery in position behind the orchestra, who would normally occupy the empty area below the stage, and on the same level as the spectators. Painting by Giovanni Pannini

All opera stems from Italy. During the Florentine Renaissance, Giovanni Bardi, Count of Vernio, and a group of musicians and intelligentsia, including Vincenzo Galilei (father of the astronomer), met at Bardi's house to try to discover a new and more human musical form. Their first experiment was based on the ancient Greek form: setting parts of plays to music and combining a single voice with a single instrument. The composers Jacopo Peri and Giulio Caccini were among the innovators.

Peri held the newly formed art of counterpoint in contempt and he and the poet Rinuccini together wrote *Dafne* 'to test the effect of the particular kind of melody which they imagined to be identical with that used by the ancient Greeks and Romans through their dramas'. *Dafne* is the first known opera, but its score is lost. It was privately performed in Florence in 1597 and it 'charmed the whole city'.

Three years later Peri composed *Eurydice*, the first true Italian opera ever to be performed in public, commissioned for the marriage festivities of King Henry IV of France and Marie de' Medici. Its orchestra, behind the scenes, consisted of a harpsichord and three stringed instruments.

Giulio Caccini used the same libretto and composed his version of *Eurydice* in similar vein. It was not performed publicly, but his action served to support Peri in launching the new music as a serious art.

At another royal marriage in Mantua in 1607, Ottavio Rinuccini provided the same libretto for *Dafne* with another called *Arianna*. This was set by Claudio Monteverdi and it caused such delight that he was commissioned to write another opera. Only one aria from *Arianna* remains, the beautiful 'Lasciatemi morire'.

For his next subject Monteverdi chose the timeless and ever fresh legend of Orpheus and Eurydice, calling it *Orfeo*. Monteverdi may not have invented the opera, but in his hands it blossomed and flourished because of his understanding of mankind coupled with his great technical skill as a composer. His orchestra had been greatly increased beyond the size of Peri's and numbered thirty-six instruments including brass, so with such variation of sonority Monteverdi began to find it possible to underline events in the story as well as to present the work with varieties of tempo and a semblance of form. He disliked the previous manner of recitative (a stylised musical speech) without any effort at relief.

No further royal marriages caused the commissioning of new operas until 1624, when Monteverdi composed his 'Intermezzo' after Orfeo, and it was not until his *Il Combattimento di Tancredi e Clorinda*, that there were any new ideas. This tragic piece was the first musical work to introduce both the pizzicato and the tremolo, two instrumental effects which have been pictorial standbys for composers ever since. Their effect at the time must have been shattering.

In 1637 two musicians opened the first public opera house in Venice entirely at their own expense. This was the Teatro di San Cassiano, where the undertaking was such a success that Monteverdi was called on to provide a new opera. This was *Adone*, first performed in 1639, and such a hit that it ran continuously for about six months. Three years later, at another new opera house in Venice, Monteverdi's masterpiece, *L'Incoronazione di Poppea* saw the light of day.

A pupil of Monteverdi's, best known by his Venetian nickname of Cavalli, proved to be a master in his own right. Melody was the mainspring of his new direction, although this was despised by Galilei and the other Florentine musical elders. Cavalli moved away from their ideals by laying the foundation for the operatic aria, because he saw the need for melody to tickle the ears of the audience and save them from the *ennui* of continuous recitative. Furthermore

Alceste *by Jean-Baptiste Lully.*
Title-page to the original score
(1674). The opera was described by
Mme. de Sévigné as 'un prodige de
beauté'

he was the first to institute the form of aria whereby the singer returns to the
first of its sections to end it (later to be called *Da Capo*). Cavalli's forty or fifty
operas include *La Calisto* and *L'Ormindo*, both of which have lately been performed at Glyndebourne and are recorded.

One of Cavalli's contemporaries, the composer Marc Antonio Cesti, provided
healthy and friendly competition, which ensured the stability and popularity
of the opera in Venice, where there were eleven opera houses before the end of
the seventeenth century. The Venetians had taken opera to their hearts so
much that they already looked upon it as their national institution.

By contrast, Rome possessed only three opera houses, and relied largely upon
importing works from Venice, towards which everybody in Italy looked for
innovation and direction, until the advent of Alessandro Scarlatti. Apart from
beginning his career in Florence and staying for a short time in Rome, Scarlatti
belonged to Naples, where he is reckoned to be the founder of the Neapolitan
School.

Opposite above: J. Périer, creator
of Pelléas in Debussy's Pelléas et
Mélisande, *Paris 1902*

Opposite below: Rowlandson's
impression of the Second Covent
Garden Theatre (1809–56). More
interesting from the point of view
of the architecture, and of the
expressions of the spectators, than
the performance of an oratorio
with organ on the stage

29

Ariadne (Mizzi Jeritza) und Zerbinetta (Margarethe Siems). Ariadne: „Sie haben mich geschmückt. Mein Grab ist da. — O meine Mutter. Jetzt geht Ariadne fort von hier." (Phot. Atelier Rembrandt, Berlin-Charlottenburg.)

He set the seal on Cavalli's aria form, naming it *Da Capo* and formulating the *recitativo secco*, in which the rhythms are sketched out by their supporting accompaniment on the harpsichord or cello, as they follow the normal accents of words. Scarlatti also invented the Italian style of overture, which begins quickly, so to judge from the 70 operatic scores which survive from his total output of some 115, Scarlatti was a great innovator.

Among several distinguished successors to Scarlatti, Domenico Freschi must be mentioned as a man who might have made a good film producer had he lived at the time of Hollywood's great years. For this opera *Bernice* he calls for:

Chorus of 100 Virgins, Chorus of 100 Soldiers, Chorus of 100 Horsemen in iron armour; 40 Cornets on horseback; 6 mounted Trumpeters; 6 Drummers; 6 Ensigns; 6 Sackbuts; 6 Flutes; 12 Minstrels, playing on Turkish and other instruments; 6 Pages, 3 Sergeants; 6 Cymbaleers; 12 Huntsmen; 12 Grooms; 12 Charioteers; 2 Lions, led by 2 Turks; 2 led Elephants; Bernice's Triumphal Car drawn by 4 Horses; 6 other Cars drawn by 12 horses; 6 Chariots, for the Procession; a Stable, containing 100 living Horses; a Forest, filled with Wild-boar, Deer and Bears.

No doubt this was all considered with great sincerity, but it seems to have more to do with the circus than the opera.

Italian opera took a somewhat different turn in 1706, when a German composer from Hamburg called George Frederick Handel came to study in Florence. His *Roderigo* was produced there and took the audience by surprise. Produc-

Ariadne auf Naxos (*1916 version: Strauss-Hofmannsthal*). In the new Prologue to this 1961 Sadler's Wells Production, the composer to a serious opera company is thrown on to the same stage as a Commedia dell'Arte troup. The Composer's delight in Zerbinetta goes some way to comforting his hurt pride. The singers are Elsie Morison and Marian Studholm (left)

tions in Venice and Rome caused equal astonishment because of the vigour of Handel's operatic talent. But 'Il caro Sassone' left Italy after only five years, considering that England would serve his cause better, although he maintained the Italian operatic idiom for the rest of his life.

The Neapolitans were the first to elevate the *intermezzi* (or interpolated musical pieces) to the level of independent works. These had started as light-hearted comments upon the main drama, which was immensely ponderous in content, and as their form altered, so the *intermezzi* eventually rose in artistic integrity to become nothing less than *opera buffa* (comical, slapstick opera). Pergolesi was the first composer to achieve this with his *La Serva Padrona* in 1734, although his output consisted of many serious works as well. He died at the age of twenty-six and his career, it has been nicely put, 'was merely a suggestion'. His fame was posthumous, but his potential was enormous. *La Serva Padrona* was received everywhere as a *succès fou*.

Perhaps we can catch a glimpse of the effect of the *intermezzo* within the same entertainment as a classical story, in the Strauss-Hofmannsthal *Ariadne auf Naxos*. Here a group of Italian clowns from the *commedia dell' arte* intervene in the story of Ariadne deserted by Theseus, and 'pep up' the interest, introduce humour and otherwise enliven what would on its own have been a static scenario.

Other composers included Niccolò Jomelli – today almost unheard – Sacchini, Paisiello and Piccini. Paisiello, a Neapolitan, composed the first *Il Barbiere di Siviglia* while Piccini was to be Gluck's most fervent rival in Paris. His compositions tend to be forgotten on account of his musico-political activities.

Domenico Cimarosa is closely associated with the *opera buffa* in his *Il Matrimonio Segreto*, which, although first performed in Vienna, is truly Italian. Cimarosa was Paisiello's rival in Naples and from the point of view of wit and gaiety he easily outpaced him; for although Paisiello's 100 or more operas are written with great facility, his style is not especially bright or sparkling.

With *opera buffa* firmly established alongside *opera seria* (but no longer intruding upon it) there seemed a need for a new master to propel the art even further forward. This was Gioacchino Rossini, large in every way, who was able to compose in both styles equally generously and equally fast. His *L'Italiana in Algeri* was composed in three weeks and was his first success with the *buffa*. It stands as an admirable example of this genre, although *Il Barbiere di Siviglia* is the prototype of comic opera in his output. Rossini's tragic opera *Otello* so upset its first audience in Naples that a happy ending had to be substituted for the Roman première to avoid the possibility of a failure there. *Semiramide* was his most ambitious opera and closed the Italian part of his career in which he had composed twenty-five operas before he reached the age of thirty-one. He then went to Paris.

Vincenzo Bellini and Gaetano Donizetti, lyrical contemporaries of Rossini, formed, in a way, the link between Rossini and Giuseppe Verdi. Bellini's *Norma* is one of the great operas of the world, his *La Sonnambula* a great achievement in melodic terms. *I Puritani* (to a feeble libretto) can still succeed, always provided that the singers are of world class.

Gaetano Donizetti's *Lucia di Lammermoor* is a great and moving tragedy based upon Scott's novel, and so possessing strong literary and dramatic backing. It requires a top-class coloratura soprano for Lucia and a persuasively lyrical tenor for Edgar (a somewhat ungrateful role). By contrast, Donizetti showed huge feeling for the comical, and among his seventy-five operas to show it best are *L'Elisir d'Amore* and *Don Pasquale*. Admittedly, Donizetti was writing for the finest voices of almost any age, and this overrode the need for versatile orchestration. But his approach, given these factors, is warm and human, while his gift for melody is inspired.

The year 1813 saw the birth of the two operatic giants of the nineteenth century: Richard Wagner and Giuseppe Verdi. From Verdi's first success, *Nabucco*, in 1842, his operas for other countries ranged widely in subject and treatment as if striving for a completely new and individual style: *I Masnadieri* for London, *Les Vêpres Siciliennes* and *Don Carlo* for Paris, *La Forza del Destino* for St Petersburg. His librettists varied from the frankly bad to the superb. Verdi referred to his composing decade of 1836–46 as 'in the galleys', but *Rigoletto* in 1851 and *La Traviata* in 1853 came as milestones in his career. *La Traviata* shows ample signs that Verdi was abandoning many of the old conventions. The revised version of *Don Carlo* is painted on a much wider and deeper canvas than the somewhat muddled *Forza*, and is a finer work. Its violent antagonisms between son and father, wife and mistress, church and state, Catholic and Protestant are subtly drawn beneath the obvious conflicts, and the score abounds in great tunes and marvellous pageantry.

Verdi's last three operas are dealt with in greater detail later in this book, for they represent his final genius, coupled with that indispensable ally to the composer: a first-class librettist.

From Verdi the Italian opera moved swiftly to the *verismo* school of which Giacomo Puccini was by far the most successful, although not the originator.

Pietro Mascagni's *Cavalleria Rusticana* of 1888 founded the movement, an opera which won first prize in a music publisher's competition. For many years this has been an almost inseparable twin in performance with Leoncavallo's *I Pagliacci*. This other *verismo* one-acter embodies the interesting feature of an *intermezzo* in which the players and stage audience become together involved when their real-life tragedy impresses itself upon the performance given by the 'fit-up' players.

Puccini's *La Bohème, La Rondine* and *Gianni Schicchi* are the only operas of the thirteen he composed which do not revel in cruelty. *Tosca* is a fine drama but fiercely sadistic; *Turandot* is harsh, and oriental in its application of exquisite torture; *Madame Butterfly* a plain story of the abandoned girl, set in Japan, and thus made more pathetic by the nature of the child-wife whose marriage applied only locally. Puccini's scores abound with the most luxurious melodies and treacly harmonies in which no effects are spared. He knew exactly what he wanted his voices to do, and while the melodic lines may be deceptively easy and go in expected directions, there is more needed than just the singing.

Ermanno Wolf-Ferrari composed four very good comic operas of which *I Quattro Rusteghi* is best known; *I Gioielli di Madonna* stands as his one essay in the *verismo* style.

Other composers like Gian Carlo Menotti (Italian-born but adopted by the United States) tried to extend Puccini's style, but only succeeded in diluting it to below the level of serious opera.

Ildebrando Pizzetti, whose operas number about twenty, is best known for his adaptation of T. S. Eliot's *Murder in the Cathedral*; Luigi Dallapiccola is the leader of the twelve-tone composers in Italy, of which *Il Prigioniero* is an effective example.

Today, Italy has no more of an idea where her opera is going than any other nation has about its own. But the originators of the opera as an art form seem generally content to listen with great pride to the singers, and to charge them with the greatest responsibility for operatic performances of which Verdi and Puccini take the lion's share.

The opera was imported into Germany from Italy in 1627 when the text for *Dafne* by Rinuccini was used in a new version to a score by Heinrich Schütz, and for a royal marriage.

Hamburg became the first city to have a resident German opera company, and this flourished under the direction of the composer Reinhard Keiser. Johan Theile's *Adam und Eva* was the first *Singspiel* (sung numbers with interpolated speech) to appear publicly in Germany in 1678. Hamburg can rightly claim to be the cradle of German opera, although there had previously been performances of Italian operas at Hamburg, as well as at Regensburg and at Munich in 1653. Keiser composed about 120 operas for Hamburg in forty years. There were about forty or fifty melodies to each, all said to be 'smooth and graceful'. They seemed to rise spontaneously from the action and to convey the sentiments of the characters. By these means, Keiser was able to make his German opera stand firmly against the declamation of the French and the pure, fine singing of the Italians.

One of the members of Keiser's orchestra had been George Frederick Handel, whose *Almira* was first performed at Hamburg in 1705. But because he favoured the Italian style more than the new German one he left Hamburg for Italy in 1706.

Johan Adolph Hasse also adopted the Italian style after considerable study in Naples and settled in Dresden for over thirty years where, between 1731 and 1763, he controlled the Italian opera and brought it to a higher artistic level than anywhere else outside Italy. Hasse composed over 100 operas but did nothing to advance the cause of German opera.

Only one of Mozart's operas received its première in Germany and that was *Idomeneo*, an *opera seria* in Italian, at Munich in 1781. The rest were first performed in Vienna and Prague.

Frederick the Great, Emperor of Prussia, was a very musical man and in order to encourage the opera in Berlin, caused the Hofoper to be built there in 1742. In 1814 Gasparo Spontini was called from Paris to be its director, and Giacomo Meyerbeer followed Spontini in 1842 with Otto Nicolai as one of his conducting staff. Nicolai's opera on the Falstaff story, *Die Lustige Weibe von Windsor*, was first produced at Berlin in 1849.

German opera was moving in several different directions and in different parts of the state that was composed of many kingdoms and palatinates, each with its opera house supported by the local monarch or duke. The development of the *Singspiel* came about in Leipzig through J. A. Hiller, first director of the Gewandhaus Concerts, who is called 'Father of the *Singspiel*'. It was a form entrenched in traditions of music based on the German *Lied*, together with spoken dialogue and orchestral numbers.

At Gotha, at the end of the eighteenth century, George Benda composed *Ariadne auf Naxos* and *Medea* in which dialogue was supported throughout by highly coloured orchestral accompaniment to heighten the tension or emphasise love scenes. This is known as 'melodrama' and its musical aspect has also been used for the cinema ever since it began.

German nationalist themes, coupled with the continuance of the Italian opera, led towards the German Romantic school. Louis Spohr's *Faust* of 1813 began it chronologically, but Carl Maria von Weber's *Der Freischütz* established it eight years later. This opera has been described as 'an embodiment of the highest ideal the romantic school is capable of realising, its truest prototype as well as its brightest ornament'.

The demands of this genre are a mixture of the romantic with the gothic; whoever the characters are, whether real or imaginary, they must always behave like ordinary beings, possessing human passions and senses. The composer must treat natural events and persons naturally but he has *carte blanche* when it comes to dealing with the supernatural. These were the rules, all faithfully obeyed by Weber, and so becoming an embodiment of what Wagner was later to attempt to achieve: the *Gesamtkunstwerk*. Spohr, on the other hand, held fast to accompanied recitative, which breaks one of the main rules of German Romantic opera and was in any case considered by his public to be 'too Italian'.

Heinrich Marschner followed Spohr and Weber, and of his six operas *Hans Heiling* is the best: about a son of the Queen of the Spirit World who loves and is rejected by a human girl. Marschner possessed everything necessary for the operatically gothic. He is seen as the natural stepping-stone between Weber and Germany's last operatic giant: Richard Wagner.

Wagner's two early works, *Die Feen* of 1833 and *Das Liebesverbot* of 1834, are seldom heard, but *Rienzi*, in five acts and something akin to Meyerbeer in shape, was produced at Dresden in 1842 and is still occasionally given though in truncated form. The canon of Wagner's operas includes *Der fliegende Höllander* (Dresden, 1843); *Tannhäuser* (Dresden, 1845); *Lohengrin* (Weimar, 1850); *Tristan und Isolde* (Munich, 1865); *Die Meistersinger* (Munich, 1868); *Der Ring des Nibelungen* in its entirety (Bayreuth, 1876) and *Parsifal* (Bayreuth, 1882). Wagner's immense vision, inventiveness, persuasion, doggedness and genius wore him out, and he died in 1883, still thinking about new operas for Bayreuth.

His mantle fell upon the shoulders of Richard Strauss, a young composer from Munich who was musically adopted for a while by Wagner's widow. He put aside direct comparison with the master by pursuing an iconoclastic path with his *Salome* and *Elektra*, but relapsed into quasi-Mozartean social comedy with *Der Rosenkavalier* (Dresden, 1911). He and Hugo von Hofmannsthal created six operas until the poet's death in 1929, after which Strauss seemed to have exhausted his inventive powers. But at the age of seventy-eight he partly wrote the libretto for his last opera, *Capriccio* (Munich, 1942), an opera about opera. His own description of himself was 'a first-class second-rate composer'. He was a modest man.

The Prague National Theatre seen from the Vltava River, where Mozart's Don Giovanni *was first performed in 1787 and his* La Clemenza di Tito *in 1791. Thereafter it became a German opera house, with Weber as its musical director between 1813 and 1817*

Apart from Hans Pfitzner, whose greatest work, though verbose, is *Palestrina*, and Ferruccio Busoni, half-German, half-Italian, but more appreciated in Germany, there is Kurt Weill, whose *Mahagonny* (1930) is a disturbing document, and Arnold Schönberg. His *Von Heute auf Morgen* was the first twelve-tone opera (Frankfurt, 1930), two operas for single characters, and the great *Moses und Aron* (Zürich, 1957). Paul Hindemith composed eight operas of which *Mathis der Maler* (Zürich, 1938) is the finest and most moving. These last three composers had to leave Nazi Germany in the mid-1930s, after which the artistic approach to opera there was a rather different matter.

Since the war, Germany's brightest operatic composer has undoubtedly been Hans Werner Henze whose *Boulevard Solitude*, a variation on the Manon story, caused great admiration when it appeared at Hanover in 1952. His *König Hirsch*, based on Goldoni (Berlin, 1956), *Der Prinz von Homburg* (Berlin, 1960), *Elegy for Young Lovers* (Schwetzingen, 1961), and *Der Junge Lord* (Berlin, 1965) all show a remarkable and truly operatic feeling for the art. Henze's most recent opera is a newly worked *Tristan und Isolde*, far removed from Wagner in musical terms yet intuitively keeping within the framework of German literature and heritage.

Vienna is unique, and must be regarded altogether separately in the history of opera. Despite the destruction of the Holy Roman Empire in 1806, whose capital had been Vienna, and of the Austro-Hungarian empire in 1918, Vienna is still a grand capital city where opera matters more than almost anything else.

The first opera to be performed in Vienna was on a favourite classical subject, *Ariadna Abbandonata*, by Bonacossi in 1641, followed by Cavalli's *Egisto*.

At the beginning of the eighteenth century, Giuseppe Galli-Bibiena designed and built two theatres to house J. J. Fux's nineteen elaborate productions supported by a large orchestra of over 130 musicians.

Model of the original Bayreuth Act II of Siegfried

Christoph Willibald Gluck was appointed Court Kapellmeister in 1754 and had ten of his operas performed in Vienna between then and 1770. When he left for Paris, the Theater am Kärntnerthor became more popular than any other since it was one of those open to the public. Three of Mozart's operas were first performed in Vienna: *Die Entführung aus dem Serail* (1782), *Le Nozze di Figaro* (1786) and *Così fan Tutte* (1790), all at the Burgtheater. His last opera to be performed – *Die Zauberflöte* – which he was too ill to hear, was scooped up by that talented jack-of-all-trades Emanuel Schikaneder, who not only presented it at his own theatre, Auf der Wieden, but wrote the libretto and played the part of Papageno.

This same Schikaneder offered Beethoven the commission to compose an opera for his theatre, and this was *Fidelio*. It was first performed there – unsuccessfully – in 1805, but later it was revised. It was revised again to emerge as one of the greatest rescue operas of all and one whose heart is so warm that it was frequently chosen to re-open opera houses in Europe after the last war.

Franz Schubert was unable to make any of his beautifully melodic operas really stand upon the stage. He composed five operettas and ten operas of which only *Die Verschworenen* (Frankfurt, 1861) is sometimes considered viable.

After Napoleon's downfall the Italians once more invaded Vienna. First Gioacchino Rossini became the most popular composer; then Gaetano Donizetti arrived to be Court Composer and Conductor. Only Albert Lortzing's *Der Waffenschmied* (1846) and Friedrich von Flotow's *Martha* (1847) actually represented German opera in Vienna, for both had their premières there.

In 1861 Wagner came to Vienna and conducted *Lohengrin* – the first time he had ever heard one of his operas in performance.

In 1869 the new Oper am Ring opened with *Don Giovanni*, and later productions included the first Viennese *Aida*. The great Austrian conductor Hans Richter became musical director of the Oper in 1893, where he mounted *Der*

Ring as well as Saint-Saëns' *Samson et Dalila*. He got together an excellent company which he yielded to Gustav Mahler when he became director in 1897. The repertoire was universal, the public interest very great. Mahler was a tyrant but he made the Vienna Hofoper into the greatest musical team of its era. His departure to America in 1907 left the organisation to a succession of directors who from that time to this have found the intrigue and the politics a deterrent to conscientious music-making.

Although the first opera to be heard in Paris is thought to have been given in early 1645 – its name and composer are unknown – *La Finta Pazzo* by Sacrati was definitely performed at the end of the same year. A few months later, a young Italian came to Paris from Florence as a page to Louis XIV's niece. His name was Giovanni Battista Lully and he is known as the father of French opera. He brought nothing of the Italian school with him, but founded a new one out of his own inspiration. He first attracted the attention of the king on account of a scurrilous song he had written, and was employed as a violinist in the royal band. From there it was easy for him to gain access to anybody of musical importance.

Lully collaborated with Jean-Baptiste Molière between 1664 and 1671, first of all in the creation of opera-ballets until in 1672 he set some verses by Philippe Quinault and created the first French opera, *Les Fêtes de l'Amour et de Bacchus*. Thereafter he and Quinault worked together on about twenty pieces. The young King Louis XIV was not at first interested in the opera at all: dance was his favourite occupation. So while Lully continued to write to please his master – and the public – he obtained from him the patent of the Academy of Music (which is still the official name for the Paris Opéra).

Lully's operas conformed to a very strict pattern within which a formal overture, accompanied recitative and well-declaimed arias were placed at dramatic and artistic moments and the whole entertainment was literally fit for a king, especially as Lully's success lay in 'a chivalrous and patriotic fidelity to the Sovereign'. The composer triumphed, and as he was far too jealous of his position to encourage anyone of equal, let alone greater, talent, he died in 1687 without leaving a musical successor in his exact style. The composer who replaced him was Jean-Philippe Rameau.

Rameau was four years old when Lully died, but not until he was in his forties did he achieve the success of *Les Indes Galantes*, in 1735. This was an opera-ballet that tells of love in four different parts of the world. It is very long, and is occasionally performed today. Rameau developed Lully's style of recitative to allow for more flexibility, and although French opera did not shed any of its formalities or ornaments, it became stronger than before. Rameau was caught up in the so-called 'Guerre des Bouffons' when Paris was divided in 1752–4 between the kind of opera which he represented and the new Italian *buffa* style which had arrived with Pergolesi's *La Serva Padrona*.

The Italian master of opera, the Viennese Christoph Willibald Gluck, arrived in Paris from Vienna in 1774 with *Iphigénie en Aulide*, written in French and produced at the Opéra. It was probably the first opera to be supported by a good public relations campaign, on account of the antagonism it aroused. But thanks to the support of the Dauphine, Marie Antoinette (Gluck's former pupil), it did succeed and Gluck was firmly established in Paris. The French opera took a new turn with productions of his earlier works, among which was his revised *Orphée*, altogether a remarkable achievement.

A composer called Niccolò Piccini led the Italian faction in Paris in denigrating everything that Gluck did. Both sides were supported by the clergy, the nobility and influential writers, and the Gluckists and the Piccinists carried their arguments into every drawing-room and café in the city. These arguments lasted until 1780 when Gluck retired to Vienna. He is said to have created cosmopolitan music by combining in his music dramas 'all the finest qualities of the Italian, and many of those in French music with the great beauties of the German orchestra'.

Piccini was unequal to the task of sustaining the future of French opera on his own, but two figures of greater stature than he to emerge after Gluck were André Grétry and Étienne Méhul who initiated the Opéra-Comique. Its demands are that the dialogue shall be spoken, not sung, and that the ending shall be a happy one. Consequently it pleased Parisian audiences on both counts and became fully established.

A Florentine called Maria Luigi Cherubini introduced himself to Paris in 1788 with *Demophon*, but it was his succeeding work *Lodoïska* – a rescue opera – that took Paris musicians by surprise. It relied on new harmonic and instrumental effects to underline dramatic events, and this technique was amply borne out by his later opera, *Medée*, in 1797. But Napoleon, who now ruled France, disliked Cherubini intensely, and because he was unlikely to prosper in such a climate, the composer went to Vienna, leaving behind him the foundation stone of the romantic opera.

By contrast, Gasparo Spontini profited from the Empress Josephine's patronage, and his *La Vestale* at the Opéra in 1807, to a text by Étienne de Juoy, brought him into full prominence as the leading opera composer of the day, indeed the 'Father' of the French Grand Opera. Probably neither Rossini nor Marschner – to quote two opposites – would have written in quite the same way had it not been for Spontini's *Fernand Cortez* of 1809. For the first time, the attributes of two opposing races, the Spanish and the Mexican, are fully exploited by the composer. This opera was revised in the most topsy-turvy manner imaginable, so that the original third act became the first, and the hero Cortez does not now appear until the second act. Planned as a political weapon to aid public feeling for Napoleon's war against the Spanish, Spontini did the reverse by making them appear noble, brave and patriotic.

In 1810 Spontini became the director of the Italian opera in Paris, and four years later he was summoned to Berlin on very good terms by King Frederick William III to improve the state of Prussian opera.

Three composers with an opera each stand out in bold relief during the following years: Daniel Auber and *Masaniello*; Giacomo Meyerbeer and *Les Huguenots*; Gioacchino Rossini and *Guillaume Tell*. Of them, Meyerbeer is the chief representative of the Grand Opera style: spectacular, large-scale, somewhat pompous and often lacking inherent musical strength, so that the work is vulnerable to any deficiency in production. Meyerbeer was greatly influenced by Rossini, and besought in vain by Weber to renounce the Italian style. Instead he partly rebuilt the French style, although Rossini's operas for Paris were far more efficiently constructed.

Daniel Auber, a Frenchman, was the first to treat the people and their hopes as the subject of an opera: considered a somewhat dangerous and revolutionary thing to do. *Masaniello* (otherwise known as *La Muette de Portici*) caused a revolt in Belgium after a performance. It is certainly a grand opera but has cause to strain the resources of the opera house when the heroine leaps from the window of her house to her death down the crater of Vesuvius!

Fromental Halévy, another Frenchman, had the good fortune to star Malibran in his first opera *Clari* in 1829, but this is now forgotten and so are most of the others that he wrote except for *La Juive* in 1835, to a libretto by the industrious Scribe.

Fortunately for Rossini, his years in Paris coincided with the reign of the

Sketch of Aloys Ander as Arnoldo in Guillaume Tell *at Covent Garden in 1852*

lavish Charles X. *Guillaume Tell* was to have been the first of five grand operas for Paris in ten years, but after the 1830 July Revolution the new king Louis-Philippe cancelled Rossini's contract and deprived France and posterity of any more operas from his pen.

Hector Berlioz was the founder of the new Romantic school of French opera. Long before Wagner he was employing a *Ring*-sized orchestra for symphonic purposes, for everything he composed was intensely dramatic in concept. But Berlioz was an anti-Wagnerian, far preferring the classic stories of ancient Greece and the imperishable works of Shakespeare. The failure of his *Benvenuto Cellini* in 1838 at the Opéra inhibited him from tackling another subject until 1856 when, for two years, he laboured over his mighty work *Les Troyens*, in five acts, telling the story from Cassandra's prophecy of Troy's doom, to the event, and the following account of Aeneas and Dido in Carthage, until his departure for Rome. It was far too unwieldy to achieve performance as he had intended it, during his lifetime, and had to be broken into two parts. If any

French opera is a direct descendant from Gluck, it is this one: immensely grand, epic and adventurous in style and presentation.

The French Opéra became established in America at New Orleans in 1859 when a new opera house was built to replace three earlier ones. At the end of the last century it was the only house in the United States to give annual and continuous seasons of opera between September and May. American premières of many French operas, from Spontini to Massenet, were given there.

Halévy's daughter had married a young composer called Georges Bizet who composed eleven operas with mixed success. His twelfth, *Carmen*, scored an instant and lasting *éclat*. First heard at the Opéra-Comique in 1875, it is said to be the greatest opera of this type. It does not exactly qualify because the end is tragic, and sometimes it is performed with recitative instead of the spoken dialogue that Bizet intended. But of the opéra-comique type it is unrivalled.

Charles Gounod's masterpiece *Faust* (1859), as well as his *Roméo et Juliette* (1867) and *Mireille* (1864), are full of charm, but neither of the last two upholds the tradition of the Grand Opera or pushes it forward. French opera merely marked time with these and other delectable bonbons. Ambroise Thomas's *Mignon* (1866) and *Hamlet* (1868) were vehicles for great singers, while Camille Saint-Saëns' emotional *Samson et Dalila* was performed outside France for fifteen years before being accepted by Paris in 1892. A pupil of Thomas, Jules Massenet, composed twenty-seven operas including *Hérodiade* (1881), *Manon* (1884), *Werther* (1892 for Vienna) and *Thaïs* (1894). Of these few, *Manon* is very likely the finest work, although *Thaïs* has lately been taken up again and has received several recordings. Massenet's *Don Quichotte* was an especial vehicle for Feodor Chaliapin in the role of the old man, but any opera presented in Paris after April 1902 must stand comparison with, and be regarded in an entirely different manner after, Claude Debussy's *Pelléas et Mélisande*.

Debussy's symbolist opera was first heard at the Opéra-Comique on 30 April 1902, an event of the utmost importance in the history of opera in general. It is probably the most original work ever to be composed for the stage, for although it is thoroughly Debussian and consequently thoroughly French (being in any case written to a French play), it employs certain Wagnerian techniques and suggestions in the orchestra. At the same time it is thoroughly anti-Wagnerian in its use of suggestion rather than insistence upon what has happened, what is happening and what may be about to happen. It is dream-like, hazy, as restrained and delicate as the best attributes of the French nation, and stands as a signpost for future composers.

Paul Dukas composed *Ariane et Barbe-Bleue* (1907) to another Maeterlinck text, and followed Debussy's pointing finger. So did Maurice Ravel in his two miniatures, *L'Heure Espagnol* (1911) and *L'Enfant et les Sortilèges* (1925), both of which are refined – though amusing.

Of the group of French composers known as 'Les Six', four composed operas. Arthur Honegger went away from Debussy by composing in a somewhat heavy and aggressive way. He was a consummate technician and understood the needs of the theatre, but in two of his works, *Le Roi David* (1921) and *Jeanne d'Arc au Bûcher*, he mixed together opera, oratorio, straight theatre, dancing and crowd-work. He seemed to be trying to do something new which was eluding him.

Darius Milhaud's *Christophe Colombe*, to a text by Paul Claudel, was produced in Berlin in 1930 and took some time to be accepted in Paris. It required many effects including film. His *David* was composed for the 3,000th anniversary of Israel and given a concert performance in Jerusalem in 1954.

The third member of 'Les Six' is Francis Poulenc whose major opera, *Les Dialogues des Carmélites*, was first heard at La Scala, Milan, in 1957. It is set in

Above left: Title page of a Farewell to Mme. Bauermeister (1849–1926), celebrated German – then British – soprano, organised by another famous soprano, Mme. Nellie Melba (1861–1931)

Right: Programme for the State visit of President Lebrun of France to England when he and his wife were guests of King George VI and Queen Elizabeth at a gala performance at Covent Garden on 22 March 1939. This 'rococo' programme was designed by Rex Whistler, and shows the trophies of France and Britain intertwined

the time of the French Revolution, with a romantic score, and tells how all the inhabitants of a Carmelite convent go to their death at the guillotine. His other two operas are very different. A *buffa* called *Les Mamelles de Tirésias* describes a couple who change sexes, while *La Voix Humaine* is a *tour de force* for a single soprano and orchestra.

Jacques Ibert wrote the inside three acts of *L'Aiglon*, and Arthur Honegger composed the outside two for Monte Carlo in 1937. Among Ibert's ten operas, a *buffa* called *Angélique* is the most successful.

Indigenous French opera now rests upon the past. The two houses in Paris are all that remain of thirty which used to present opera all the time in the 1920s. Opera and operetta, to be exact. But the glory of operetta is another story altogether.

While the opera stemmed from the drama in Italy and the ballet in France, it progressed naturally from the masque in England. Henry Purcell, one of the greatest of musical innovators, brought the age of the masque to a close by his introduction of the opera. His – regrettably – single work, *Dido and Aeneas* (1689 or 1690), has such completeness, depth and fulfilment that it was far ahead of the struggling Italian opera of the time. That Purcell devoted far more time to writing incidental music to plays is a great loss for which the existence of *Dido and Aeneas* goes some way to compensating.

In 1711, at the Queen's Theatre in the Haymarket, an opera called *Rinaldo* appeared, composed by an unknown German called George Frederick Handel. It was considered to be the finest opera that had ever been heard on account of its beautiful arias. There was still some of the previously mentioned 'circus' treatment when a flock of live birds was released during a pertinent orchestral interlude, and this impurity underlined another: a mixture of the English and Italian languages.

Handel's opposition, troubles, failures, successes, rivalry with the Italian composer Bononcini, and difficulties with the temperamental castrati, needing enormous patience, courage and physical strength, all went on for thirty years in London. Handel died there in poor health and reduced circumstances eighteen years later, but he will remain one of the pillars of the opera in England. He was a prime exponent of the *opera seria* but was unable to divest it of its own limitations, and so turned to oratorio instead. This he almost turned into opera, so vividly and dramatically did he envisage and execute his oratorios – even to stage directions.

Joseph Haydn offers a resemblance to Purcell. His one opera for London, composed but not performed because of a change in the theatre's management, is *Orfeo ed Euridice*. It is more refined than dramatically exciting, and was the only example of a Haydn opera for a large theatre and not for the constricting demands of Prince Esterházy's minute private one.

During Handel's 'reign' in London the Italian *opera seria* was the only kind to be found on the stage, and even so-called English works were still advertised as being performed 'in the Italian style' – in other words, with recitative in place of dialogue – until 1728. In this year John Gay and Dr Pepusch produced their *Beggar's Opera* in which the dialogue was spoken but the music was mainly folk tunes from England and Scotland, and a march from Handel's *Rinaldo*. It was the original ballad opera, and a rousing success. The speed and number of imitations by Arne, Storace, Dibdin and others continued through the eighteenth century until Sir Henry Bishop diluted the form and robbed it of its former spontaneity.

Two Irishmen and an English-naturalised German each composed an opera which together were slightingly known as 'The English Ring': Vincent Wallace's *Maritana* (1845), Michael Balfe's *Bohemian Girl* (1843) and Sir Julius Benedict's *Lily of Killarney* (1862). The nineteenth century was the century of oratorio in England: her successive Masters of the Queen's Music were not opera composers. All works for the stage were imported with a few exceptions like Frédéric D'Erlanger's *Tess*.

From 1910 until 1939, the Royal Opera House, Covent Garden, was run, generally during the summer season, by various syndicates. The most famous impresario was Sir Thomas Beecham whose family fortune helped to keep the opera going in spite of heavy losses. Beecham introduced several composers' operas to London in his first season, Richard Strauss, Ethel Smyth and notably Frederick Delius. This English-born composer of German parentage who lived most of his life in France produced one masterpiece, *A Village Romeo and Juliet*, which was heard twice then, and three times in 1920. It has received several more performances since the Second World War, and so has another Delius opera, *Koanga* (first heard at Covent Garden in 1935). It was not until after the Second World War when the state intervened and, through the Arts Council, helped to support Covent Garden, that a new ensemble was built up and a variety of policies introduced.

Between 1931 and 1939, a somewhat homespun English-language opera company was run at the Sadler's Wells Theatre, having moved there from Lilian Baylis's Old Vic in the Waterloo Road. It was here at Sadler's Wells in 1945 that

A Midsummer Marriage (*Tippett.*
Covent Garden 1955). This picture,
from the revival in 1968, shows
Alberto Remedios as Mark, Joan
Carlyle as Jenifer, the body of
Raimund Herincx as King Fisher
and Stafford Dean as the Priest

English opera got up on its feet again and proclaimed itself still living with
Peter Grimes, the first successful opera by Benjamin Britten.

Sir Arthur Bliss's *The Olympians*, Sir William Walton's *Troilus and Cressida*
– and later *The Bear* – and Sir Michael Tippett's four operas to date (*A Midsummer Marriage*, *King Priam*, *The Knot Garden* and *The Ice-Break*), all in the
romantic vein, if, in Tippett's case, they are such personal works as to be partly
incomprehensible without a great deal of study.

Of the 'modernists', Richard Rodney Bennett, Gordon Crosse, Elisabeth
Lutyens, Nicholas Maw and John Taverner have each had operas staged, but
it is too early to say how bright the prospect of English opera is going to be.

Certainly, as an art, it flourishes in Britain as never before, with Glynde-
bourne going strong (since 1934), Opera North, the Welsh National and Scottish
Opera becoming recognised as firmly and truly based, and the English National
Opera (formerly Sadler's Wells) now commissioning works as well as staging
Der Ring, but as *The Ring*. Rising costs bedevil the opera almost more than any
other art, because the opera has to be grand, luxurious and glorious.

Opera in the United States began with folk opera, and now it encourages a
strong resurgence of national themes. In between – and even now at most of the
large opera houses – the accent has been upon the great romantic operas from
Europe as well as visits from foreign singers.

The Beggar's Opera, with its political satire at the expense of King George II and his government, arrived speedily in New York in 1751; *Love in a Village*, Arne's pastiche and folk opera, arrived in 1768, moving to Boston in 1769. But the first American opera appears to have been *Tammanny or The Indian Chief* which received its première in New York in 1794. A French resident there called Pellesier composed scores to librettos by Dr Smith of Connecticut at the turn of the eighteenth century, including adaptations of Rossini's *Il Barbiere* and Mozart's *Il Nozze di Figaro*.

New York's musical public were thus prepared for, although no doubt surprised and delighted by, the first season of Italian opera which was given at the Park Theater on 26 November 1825 with the real *Il Barbiere* sung by the Garcia family. French opera was also introduced there, and the German repertoire came to Niblo's Gardens on 16 September 1856 with Meyerbeer's *Robert der Teufel*.

Up to 1854 the Academy of Music (on the north-east corner of Irving Place and 14th Street) was the only considerable house for the presentation of grand opera in New York. It had opened on 2 October 1854 with *Norma*, and US premières of Verdi's and other Italian operas followed. But a group of opera-loving New York businessmen who were excluded from the chance of renting private boxes at the Academy put up $800,000 and built a rival house which they called the Metropolitan Opera. It stood on Broadway between 39th and 40th Streets and became known as the Diamond Horseshoe. It became the setting for the world's greatest singers from its opening on 22 October 1883 with *Faust* until it closed its doors for ever on 16 April 1966 and transferred to the new Lincoln Center.

After a financially shaky start, the Met was managed from 1898 by Maurice Grau, who set it on its feet. He imported the finest German singers from Europe as guests and the enterprise prospered. From 1903 to 1908 Heinrich Conried took over from Grau and brought Caruso to New York as well as Gustav Mahler to conduct. He was then superseded by Giulio Gatti-Casazza, lured from the managership of La Scala, Milan, who was to have the most influential effect on the well-being of the Met for the next twenty-seven years. He mounted 177 operas in this time, in more than 5,000 performances, and it was through his skill in attracting the best singers, musicians and personnel and in his internal strategy that the Met became world-famous. Gatti-Casazza could literally summon any artists in the world – and pay what they asked.

Toscanini was the Met's chief conductor of the Italian repertoire between 1908 and 1915. Between the wars he was in Italy again, though not always at La Scala, but with the emergence of the Fascists in his native land he returned to the United States. He was invaluable to the Met, not as a conductor, but because with the NBC Symphony Orchestra he used certain Met singers for his broadcasts, recordings and concert performances of operas. Among them were the sopranos Licia Albanese and Herva Nelli, the mezzo Nan Merriman, the tenor Jan Peerce, the baritone Robert Merrill and the bass Nicola Moscona. He welded these into an ensemble for the recordings they made together.

From 1935 to 1950 Edward Johnson, a Canadian tenor who had been a singing member of the Met Company since 1922, became manager. He was followed by the redoubtable Rudolf Bing from Vienna, Darmstadt, Berlin, Glyndebourne and the Edinburgh Festival. Bing wouldn't stand any nonsense from anybody.

The New Met in the Lincoln Center opened with Samuel Barber's *Antony and Cleopatra*, an all-American opera starring Leontyne Price.

While the Met is probably the most internationally famous of North American opera houses, and indeed of any in the world, it does not necessarily represent the whole of the United States. At the City Center in New York the opera company which was founded by Mayor La Guardia in 1941 experienced similar teething troubles to the Met in its early days. It settled down under its musical director Julius Rudel after 1957. This company concentrates on a reasonable proportion of American operas and in giving opportunities to graduate singers from the schools of music, of which the Juilliard School is one of the foremost and specialises in operas sung in English.

San Francisco's Opera lies closer to the Met in prestige than any other US company. It began in 1852 when a touring company brought Bellini's *La Sonnambula*. The present company, founded in 1923, has attracted many star singers who quite often seem satisfied with singing there and not necessarily at the Met too. The War Memorial Opera House was opened on 15 October 1932 with *Tosca*, at a time when there was an emphasis on the Italian repertoire. But in the 1940s, owing to the availability of refugees from Germany such as Lotte Lehmann and Friedrich Schorr, as well as Kirsten Flagstad and Lauritz Melchior, the Wagnerian operas had stronger casts than ever before.

The Chicago Opera also began in 1852 after a touring company (the same one?) had brought *La Sonnambula* on 29 July 1850. The Crosby Opera House was built in 1865 and flourished until it was burnt down in 1871. The Chicago Auditorium was built to replace it and opened its doors in 1889 with Gounod's *Roméo et Juliette*. Visiting companies were welcome there whenever they came anywhere near, but played for only a few weeks at a time until 1910. In this year the Chicago Grand Opera Company was formed and launched itself on 3 October 1910. Mary Garden, the Scottish soprano who had created the role of Mélisande in Debussy's opera in Paris, sang there until 1931. In the season 1921–2 she was made General Director and managed to lose $1m, but gave the world première of Serge Prokofiev's fantastic fairy-tale opera *The Love of Three Oranges*. The new Civic Opera Company opened with *Aida* on 4 November 1929 but went bankrupt during the Depression. From then until after the Second World War, only visiting companies appeared in Chicago but with international stars such as Maria Callas, Birgit Nilsson and Tito Gobbi.

So far as compositions are concerned, America has many of her own operas to be proud of. They start with Hewitt's *Tammanny*, performed at the John Street Theater, but of which nothing has been handed down. Some parts of the score of *The Archers or Mountaineers of Switzerland* do exist, and show it to be based on the William Tell story. It was first performed on 18 April 1796 in New York to a score by an Englishman called Benjamin Carr.

In 1896 Walter Damrosch, a German emigré conductor and composer, brought out his original opera *The Scarlet Letter*. This was followed in 1913 by *Cyrano de Bergerac* and three other operas. Deems Taylor's *The King's Henchman* was given at the Met in 1926, as a result of which he was commissioned by the opera house to write a new work for them. This was *Peter Ibbetson*, which had its première on 7 February 1931 with Edward Johnson as the leading tenor.

Virgil Thompson was a pupil of Nadia Boulanger and was also a friend of Gertrude Stein. Their *4 Saints in 3 Acts* was produced in 1928, followed by their second collaboration, *The Mother of Us All*, on 7 May 1937. (Mr Thompson was the senior music critic of the *New York Times* between 1940 and 1954.) Another pupil of Nadia Boulanger, also of Arnold Schönberg, was Marc Blitzstein, who decided to abandon musical experimentation and to compose with lyricism and a direct approach to the audience. *The Cradle will Rock* (1937) and *Regina* (1949) emphasise this.

Douglas Moore developed the American theme with *The Ballad of Baby Doe* in 1956, which had been preceded by *The Devil and Daniel Webster*. Lukas Foss's *The Jumping Frog of Calaveras County* (1950) was another folk opera based on a story by Mark Twain.

George Gershwin's *Porgy and Bess* has been called 'the American National Opera'. It had its world première at Boston on 30 September 1935 and its tunes became well known all over the world. Its first production outside the USA was, surprisingly enough, in Copenhagen in 1943, during the Nazi occupation. *Porgy* was first heard in London when an American company touring Europe with it brought it to the Stoll Theatre on 9 October 1953. Leontyne Price as Bess was making her London début.

In 1941 Benjamin Britten was in New York and composed *Paul Bunyan*, to a libretto by W. H. Auden, which was performed at Columbia University but was withdrawn and remained unpublished and unheard until 1 February 1976 when it received its first hearing (broadcast by the BBC) in Europe. It turned out to be a true American folk-morality opera.

Samuel Barber's first opera was *Vanessa* which was performed at the Met in 1958 and then given three performances at that year's Salzburg Festival, in English. Apart from *Porgy and Bess* it is probably the only national American opera to have been performed in Europe.

Above: Vanessa (Barber–Menotti). *Scene from Act IV of the première at the Metropolitan Opera, New York in 1958 showing Eleanor Steber as Vanessa (far left), Rosalind Elias as Erika (being carried), Regina Resnik as the Baroness (back to camera) and Nicolai Gedda as Anatol. The costumes are by Cecil Beaton*

Porgy and Bess. *European tour of revival 1953–4 showing the fight between Porgy (William Warfield) and the villainous Crown, whom Porgy kills out of jealousy for Bess*

III La Donna è Mobile

Opposite: Lilli Lehmann (1848–1929). One of the most celebrated and 'comprehensive' German sopranos of the second half of the nineteenth century, singing 170 roles in French and Italian, as well as in German, in nearly 120 operas. Sang in the first Bayreuth Ring, and made her Met début as Carmen

Below: Maria Callas and Renato Cioni as Tosca and Cavaradossi after the torture scene in Act II of Tosca. Callas's powers of characterisation are expressed to the full here

50

*A*n operatic *prima donna* is notoriously temperamental but of great stature, character, personality and glamour. So are the other voices: the mezzo-sopranos, contraltos, tenors, baritones and basses. But the soprano has achieved the glory of being the most outrageous.

She is usually the heroine of an opera, the voice that is 'on top', but merely to call her a soprano is not enough. The exact kind needs description. In *Fidelio*, for instance, the only solo female voices are both sopranos, Leonore herself, the heroine of the opera, who must possess a heavy dramatic voice suitable to the ardours of her experience in the prison; and the young Marcelline, a pretty little thing, who is a light soprano. From the moment they open their mouths they give themselves away – in the best possible manner. From the way in which they sing you could not mistake one for the other.

A soprano is typed by her vocal strength, range, quality and agility, and it is no exaggeration to say that there is an operatic part already written for any voice today. This is why, when an exceptional or unusual voice comes along, some old and forgotten opera is taken off the shelf, dusted and revived as a vehicle for Mme So-and-So's amazing technique. Very few sopranos attempt to sing roles that fall right across the whole vocal range of the operatic repertoire, but from time to time it nearly happens. In the past, so the musical history books say, there were sopranos who could sing a number of totally unrelated roles – unrelated, that is, for the voice one would have expected to cope with only one or two of them.

In the last century Lilli Lehmann (whom Wagner cast in three roles for the first Bayreuth *Ring* in 1876), also sang Carmen, Violetta and Lucia. This kind of versatility has again happened in living memory in the person of Maria Callas. She sang the heavy roles of Isolde and Brünnhilde when a young woman in Italy, later she tackled the florid Bellini characters, then Norma, Medea, Violetta and Lucia. But while Mme Lehmann kept her voice in good order, Mme Callas wore hers out and cut short her career before she was fifty. She appeared last of all as Tosca. At this age one can expect a soprano to continue for at least another ten years, probably in the heavier roles; for with increasing age the voice tends to become richer (as with experience) and to incline in quality away from the top. The singer can easily shift the emphasis of her repertoire downwards as Kirsten Flagstad did, recording a lovely Fricka instead of the expected Brünnhilde.

Apart from these stalwart ladies who have to appear perfectly well able to look after themselves, there are the paler, feebler sopranos dying of consumption (Violetta, Mimi); those in the grip of fate and unable to move a step unless it is preordained (Mélisande, Leonora (*Forza*), Electra, Judith (*Bluebeard's Castle*)). Eternal Woman is to be found in Mozart's operas: Donnas Anna and Elvira (*Don Giovanni*), Fiordiligi and Dorabella (*Così*), Pamina, Papagena and the Queen of Night in *Die Zauberflöte*. This last role is a highly ornamented one called *coloratura*, meaning coloured, and one demanding a rapid, twiddly kind of singing, the remnant of a bygone age. But Mozart wrote this part with a particular soprano in mind, although his genius took it further in underlining her brittle temperament in this kind of music – psychological casting. Apart from Papagena, Mozart also remembered the lesser kind of Eternal Woman: Blondchen (*Entführung*) and Despina (*Così*), faithful servants whose native wit often enables them to achieve far more than their masters and mistresses.

Sopranos have a fairly clear field among operatic heroines, but mezzo-sopranos are not altogether excluded from the star roles, whether as heroine or anti-heroine or as a subordinate character with whom we end up by sharing full sympathy. Carmen is the finest leading mezzo role, for it gives the singer a wide range of opportunities in characterisation, acting and vocal panache. The

Adelina Patti in costume of Aïda *as worn at the London première of Verdi's opera in 1876 at Covent Garden. The diva 'displayed not only that superb vocalisation for which she has long been renowned but also those largely enhanced powers of tragedy and tragic expression . . .'*

sort of sympathy which Carmen evokes in the listener is of an unusual kind, because she is a kind of witch. No wonder poor Don José was captivated – and ruined – by her. Rossini composed two operas for a coloratura mezzo, *La Cenerentola* (Cinderella), whose voice is purposely contrasted with those of her soprano ugly sisters, and *L'Italiana in Algeri*, a comedy role. Rosina in *Il Barbiere* was also written for this kind of voice, but, as it was difficult to find, Rossini allowed a soprano for the second production, since when a soprano has become the rule. A pity, though, for the mezzo Rosina, when she can be heard, seems to make all the other characters fall vocally into place more neatly.

Verdi's *Aida* has two princesses in the leading female roles; the Ethiopian Aida is a soprano and the Egyptian Amneris is a mezzo. Aida has no noticeable strength of character apart from true love for her tenor hero, Radamès, but Amneris is a real woman: fierce, proud, jealous, strong and as much in love with Radamès herself. While he is being tried for treason, Amneris has a magnificent scene alone, outside the council chamber from which she (and we) can hear the questioning and the judgement. Her plea for clemency makes this the finest scene in the opera.

In another triangle of passion, the Druid High Priestess, Norma (in Bellini's opera) finds herself unwittingly betrayed by her closest friend, Adalgisa. The man in question is a Roman, consequently a national enemy, who is playing fast and loose with them both. Adalgisa does not attract as much sympathy as Norma, but she performs a very important musical function in her duets and trios and dramatically as well by supporting Norma in her hour of greatest need. She has a duet with Norma that was at one time considered very tiresome (it is all in thirds) but which is considered today to be one of the 'show-stoppers'.

Occasionally a soprano or a mezzo has to dress up as a young man and take a 'breeches-role' to its extreme by assuming his sex. The most famous of these are Cherubino in *Figaro* (the original of the genre); Oscar in *Ballo* and Siebel in *Faust*, both sopranos; Octavian in *Der Rosenkavalier*, Prince Orlofsky in *Die Fledermaus* and Nicklausse in *Les Contes d'Hoffmann* – all mezzos. By giving these roles to women, so as to obtain a soprano or mezzo voice, the composers may have had something else in mind. In 1787, when *Figaro* was first produced, Cherubino must have been an extraordinary sex symbol. To see a woman's legs in public was a rare event, and Mozart recognised that such titillation was bound to put visual emphasis upon Cherubino's character in exactly the way in which he wanted him/her to appear. This consideration was of less weight when Strauss's Octavian was first seen, but both these characters have – in the course of their opera plots – to change sexes again, thus becoming a girl dressed up as a boy dressed up as a girl.

These parts are all similar to the old pantomime principal boy, but all completely different from the serious breeches-role of Leonore in *Fidelio*. She is known to the audience all along as being a woman in disguise, although sometimes it is difficult to understand how the singer's build can allow her to get away with it. Two other characters who are forced to adopt male disguise are the other Leonore in *Forza* and Gilda in the last act of *Rigoletto*. These two operas are tragedies, and since *Fidelio* was all but a tragedy too, the serious *Hosenrollen* seem to be quite another matter – except for one: Zdenka in *Arabella*. But there is quite an unusual *frisson* here when she is dressed as a boy and receives a man in bed in total darkness, pretending that she is her sister Arabella.

Mozart's *Zauberflöte* requires nine sopranos of different voices, in groups of three. As the opera is based on freemasonry, its symbolic aspect adds to an interesting and varied use of character through vocal casting. There is Pamina, a pure young girl; her hysterical mother the Queen of Night; and Papagena, a

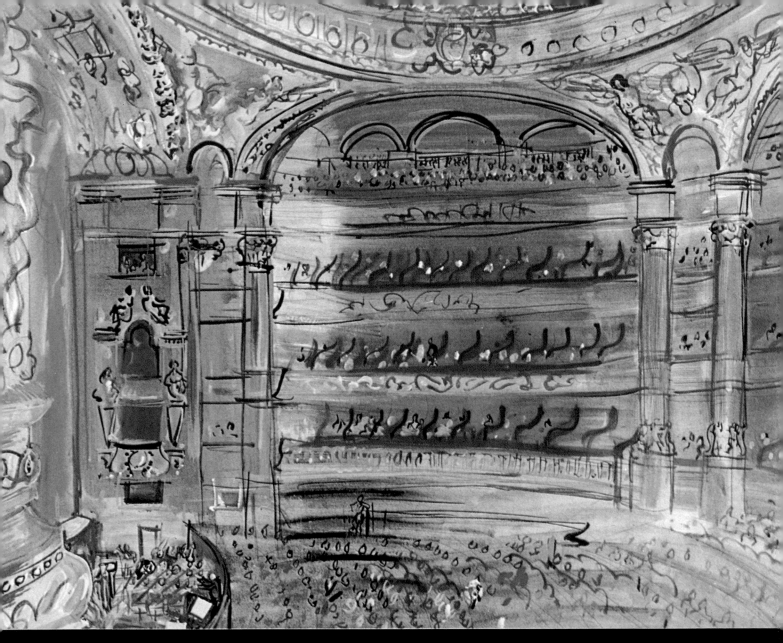

Le Nozze de Figaro (Mozart–da Ponte, Vienna 1786). Teresa Berganza as Cherubino and Sir Geraint Evans as Figaro in Act I. Costume design by Erni Tnietert, set design by Tio Otto. Covent Garden 1963

Inset: Teresa Berganza as Cherubino going off to be a soldier

Opposite: Fitting an awkward costume to a singer on the set, where her requirements to move up and down a flight of steps, and to raise her arms, are being met by two seamstresses under the costume designer's guidance

sprightly little bird-woman. Besides these three principals there are three Ladies and three Boys (soprano, soprano, contralto in both cases).

Three merry wives, Mistresses Page, Ford and Quickly, and Nanetta Page are the four women principals in Verdi's *Falstaff*. Quickly stands apart from the others with her deep, luscious, fruity voice that twice lures Falstaff to humiliation and ridicule. Such jolly parts for 'elderly' mezzos hardly ever occur, in fact Mistress Quickly seems to stand at the opposite pole to Erda in *Der Ring*, a contralto who is another oracle of disaster.

The contralto voice is the darkest and rarest in the female range, usually given to nurses, confidantes, fortune-tellers, witches and harridans. Characters such as Orfeo or Idamante in *Idomeneo*, sung today by contraltos, were not intended for women's voices at all. The composers wrote them for castrati, a phenomenon that held the opera stage during most of the eighteenth century, and subordinated sopranos and real male voices to little more than supporting roles. By what has been politely called 'a barbarous operation' on a boy before his voice had broken, his voice was preserved and became strong with manhood. It then possessed the range and purity of a boy's, coupled with the strength and volume of a man's. From contemporary accounts the castrati's voices, soprano or alto, were surprisingly beautiful if handled with proper artistic feeling, but this was seldom the case because of the castratis' inordinate vanity. They were pampered and idolised by their audiences and always took roles of gods, kings or ancient heroes. In the present century we get only a vague impression of what this high, male voice sounded like by hearing counter-tenors. In his *Midsummer Night's Dream* opera, Benjamin Britten has cast Oberon for a counter-tenor, emphasising the ethereal quality of the King of the Fairies. But it is unlikely that any counter-tenor possesses the necessary technique or years of training which would enable him to compete with the vocal acrobatics which were the castratis' stock-in-trade.

Today's operatic hero is usually a tenor. The conventional portrait of a vain, tubby little man is not necessarily correct any longer. Tenors play the handsome lovers, the gallant young princes and dukes, the young kings, the cads and the dupes. They vary from the *tenore di grazia* like Almaviva in *Il Barbiere*, to the massive Wagnerian *Heldentenor* (heroic tenor) of *Siegfried*. They hardly sound like the same voice at all, indeed they are not, yet they are both classified as tenors. The weightiest Italian tenor role is Otello which, Caruso said, should never be attempted by a singer under the age of fifty. He was studying it himself and had recorded three numbers from it when he died in 1921 at the age of forty-eight. At least two tenors in recent years, having ignored Caruso's advice, have been put permanently out of business by this huge role, which demands that the tenor has graduated from baritone, otherwise he has not the necessary support which enables him 'to sing on the interest, never on the capital' of the voice. This is all the more true of Wagnerian tenors, especially in such an arduous role as Tristan. One recalls a performance of this opera where there seemed to have been a great deal of capital depreciation, for a different singer appeared in each of the three acts.

Recorded versions of operas can be deceptive over the way in which singers are cast in a variety of roles that they could never manage from the stage. The microphone makes many things possible. Such a 'portmanteau' tenor as Nicolai Gedda seems to be able to accomplish wonders with a repertoire that goes halfway across the board from Arnold in *Guillaume Tell* to Rodolfo in *La Bohème* and Count Almaviva, via the Tenor Singer in *Der Rosenkavalier*. This latter role is rather odd. Strauss's opera has no leading tenor because the hero is a breeches-role. In any case Strauss strongly disliked the tenor voice and so this arrangement suited him admirably. But the one tenor of musical importance in the opera (though he has none in the plot) has to sing and mimic an 'Italian Serenade' that is extraordinarily difficult, although there is nothing really Italian about it. The words are by Molière and the puzzling accompaniment and melody are pure Strauss.

French tenors are something else again. They are found to be either strong, romantic heroes such as Raoul in Meyerbeer's *Les Huguenots* or as Arnold in Rossini's *Tell*, all the surer by coming out of national histories. Berlioz calls for a real heroic tenor in *Les Troyens* for Aeneas, and a honey-sounding lyric tenor for Hylas in his song about the bees. But there are many requirements for exceptional voices in this opera from France's greatest composer before Debussy.

The next kind of classic French tenor is Faust in Gounod's opera, and Roméo in the same composer's later work. Don José in *Carmen* is more an extension of Aeneas than of Gounod's lovelorn heroes, although the extremes of passion that he encounters are tougher and cruder than any before. All these are moody and passionate lovers, and so is the last, Pelléas. This role calls for a refined singer who is also a strong actor, able to convey the character's sense of fate.

The traditional and conventional vocal quartet is composed of soprano, mezzo, tenor and bass, like four-part harmony, but the most famous quartet in all opera uses a baritone instead of a bass voice at the bottom. The opera is *Rigoletto*, and the quartet employs a nice feeling for dramatic irony where the owners of the top and bottom voices are peeping in to a house where the middle voices are unaware of them. But they all sing together in perfect harmony. The baritone role of Rigoletto lies rather high, and while such singers as Tito Gobbi, Leonard Warren, Marko Rothmuller and Sherrill Milnes have tackled the role, Geraint Evans found it too high for him. Rigoletto is a tricky part to act because it treads the tightrope between comedy and tragedy, rather as Wozzeck does in Alban Berg's opera of that name.

Right: Hans Richter (1843–1916). Austro-Hungarian conductor assistant to Wagner in 1866-7; conducted the first Bayreuth Ring *in 1876; and the first* Ring, Tristan *and* Meistersinger *in London. Attempted, in vain, to found an English National Opera*

Below: Carmen. *Shirley Verrett as Carmen being menaced by Placido Domingo (Don José) before he stabs her to death outside the bull ring in the last act. Covent Garden 1973*

In *Don Giovanni* there are three baritones, the Don, Leporello and Masetto. The creator of the Don had a voice that the French call *bariton-Martin*, a very high, nearly tenor voice named after the first singer to possess one. (Pelléas is sometimes sung by a *bariton-Martin* rather than a tenor – depending on availability.) In spite of this, the Don is sometimes sung today by a real bass, and this would seem to throw the vocal balance between the three baritones completely askew. Masetto should have the deepest voice of the three, and between them is Leporello.

The baritone voice quite often signifies an operatic villain, of which Scarpia (*Tosca*) and Don Pizarro (*Fidelio*) are probably the vilest. Verdi's fathers are always baritones and there is often a father–daughter duet, in which the girl is always a soprano. Baritone–tenor duets tend to be between two men swearing a vow of friendship (*Don Carlos*, *Götterdämmerung*, *Forza*, *Otello*).

Wagner's great insight into vocal casting persuaded him to cast both his principals in the fight between evil and good in *Der Ring*, Alberich and the god Wotan, as bass-baritones. This is a voice of great nobility and sonority combined with fluency so that it is able to negotiate melodious passages as well as declamatory ones.

Basses are the voices which portray the Devil, Russian princes, troubled kings devoid of sexual aspiration, an occasional eunuch, conspirators, assassins and nearly all imposing dignitaries. Probably the most humorous and likeable bass character, although a bit of a rogue, is Baron Ochs in *Der Rosenkavalier* who ends the second act with an E below the bass stave, and it must be a fat E, prolonged and audible. Most Western basses find anything down here to be awkward territory, but Russian and other Slavonic basses are somehow able to get even lower, and without loss of quality or volume. Although he has no *basso profundo* notes to sing, Boris Godunov in Mussorgsky's opera is one of the most challenging bass-acting parts, combining a need for proper dignity with gradual mental deterioration. In Verdi's *Rigoletto* there is a very good duet for baritone (Rigoletto) and bass, Sparafucile, a common assassin who also keeps a bawdy house. It is a conversation between the two men when Sparafucile offers his knife for hire whenever the jester may need it. But, exciting though this is, the best bass scene is between two basses in *Don Carlos*. They are the Grand Inquisitor and King Philip II, representing Church and State – and they come into collision. Over a dragging motif in the brass, which expresses the inexorability of the Inquisitor, he gets his own way with the King. And the fact that he is blind makes it even more gripping.

Chaliapin was probably the most famous bass singer in Europe and America between the two world wars, and he excelled not only in *Boris Godunov*, but also as a drunken monk called Varlaam in the same opera which he sometimes used to double. Other roles were the half-crazed Don in Massenet's *Don Quichotte* and Mefistofele in Boito's opera where his whistling, half-naked epitome of evil was a vivid characterisation.

There is yet another kind of voice which can be used throughout the whole range from soprano to bass on the opera stage, and that is the speaking voice. Opera singers are notoriously bad at speaking ordinarily in those operas which require dialogue between the sung numbers: *Carmen*, *Fidelio*, *Entführung*, *Zauberflöte* and many of the lighter *Singspiels*. In the confines of the stage there is nothing that can be done by way of a deputy to say the lines, although in gramophone recordings this is generally done with actors speaking and singers singing. In the *Entführung*, one character, the Bassa Selim, has no singing at all, and an actor invariably takes him on. Carl Ebert used to play him with great success. Speaking singers generally give away some undesirable provincial or foreign accent, or else they possess a normal voice which conflicts with

59

the personality that their singing voice has acquired. No, Salome may send on a deputy from the ballet to negotiate the Dance of the Seven Veils for her, but Carmen is obliged to sing, dance and speak throughout her role.

One thing seems clear today, when looking back on the years before the First World War, and to a modified extent between the wars: singers kept their voices for much longer than they seem able to today. There are several reasons for this. Up to 1914, the world moved at a leisurely pace, singers took their time over their training and, later on, in travelling from one place to another. There was no state-aided opera with pension schemes and security of appointment. Each house was supported either by a monarch or an impresario who demanded only the best. There was consequently no room for passengers and only the most hard-working or outstanding artists could expect to keep pace, let alone to succeed, for the competition between excellent voices and tough personalities was fierce. Most important of all, that deterrent to the well-being of the voice and all prospects of an enduring career, the aeroplane, did not exist as a conventional means of transport.

But today it is quite a different story. The singer dashes home after a performance in one place, gets up early the next morning and flies to the next engagement, perhaps even on to a third within ten days. While this may be a partial exaggeration if applied to all our leading singers today, it certainly fits some of them, so it is no wonder that few can sustain careers of half the length of their predecessors. Their voices are subjected to constant use, inadequate rest and the additional grievance of air travel.

It is not uncommon for a singer to get off the aeroplane delayed by fog, to be met by a member of the musical staff of the opera house in a taxi. He will be armed with photographs and plans of the sets which the singer will attempt to absorb on the way to the opera house for the performance *that evening*, while the vehicle is constantly being held up in traffic jams. What a way to prepare for an appearance!

To become an opera singer needs no social background, no intellect, no family riches (though they can be useful), no especially good looks. It all depends upon a double gift at birth: a voice and intelligence. A child's singing comes naturally at first, and little harm can come to it; after that the gift has to be recognised, and even if there is parental obstruction, the determined singer-to-be will overcome it, whatever the reasons that are put up. The next step is hard work, and this will go on for ever. Unlike any other kind of musician, there is no expensive instrument to buy, it is all there, waiting to be developed and trained. It is a glorious gift in pursuit of a glorious career.

It is very important indeed to find the right teacher, and there is no hard and fast method of ensuring that pupil and teacher are matched. Even if the pupil has to find a new master, which sometimes happens, and it means a certain amount of re-learning, adaptation and what will seem a hold-up in progress, it is sometimes a necessary step to take. But chopping and changing because of impatience is not to be considered. With all this there never comes a time when the singer has finished learning; once begun, the art of singing is a study, even as a teacher after retirement from active work in the opera house or on the concert platform. So it should be with every art. Dancers, even more than singers, have to discipline themselves to morning class every day. There was a time when Margot Fonteyn could be seen working under the guidance of a famous teacher in a West End back-street studio in London, side by side with, and receiving criticism with, members of the *corps de ballet*. Here is an example of complete subjection of personality and person to the art.

The training of singers in most American and European cities is by means of recognised schools and academies, then on to a specialist opera school, of which possibly only a few will exist in each country. Competition to enter these is fierce, and the training differs from one to another. Some American universities have faculties of music which include opera. The whole process may take up to five or even seven years (including post-graduate courses) and includes a degree in case the student is forced to turn to teaching as a last resort. He will thus possess a paper qualification. A good voice may help to gain admittance to a singing school: the most vivid imagination alone will not. But without this, the voice lacks one vital adjunct that will turn singer into opera singer and cagebird into *rara avis*.

Then begins a kind of interim period, a living in suspense, when the singer either promotes himself at a concert, attends auditions conscientiously, or both. An opportunity is the great thing. And with a good teacher's advice and encouragement, the singer will gain and pass the audition. Choice of aria and of dress should always be considered in an objective manner, for the panel will not be *waiting* for any particular singer to appear: each is merely a number, another one to get over and done with in a hard and irritating morning's work.

In 1918 the Metropolitan Opera had scheduled Verdi's *La Forza del Destino* for production and Caruso would sing in it. But no Leonora had been cast. The tenor had heard a remarkable young woman of not quite twenty-two who had studied with two reputable teachers after appearing in vaudeville. Her name was Rosa Ponselle. The director of the Metropolitan Opera, Gatti-Casazza, was very doubtful but agreed to audition her. Instead of singing an aria from the opera in question, she sang the long scena for Norma in Act I of Bellini's opera, quite one of the most difficult pieces of singing and a distinctly hazardous choice for an audition. But she sang it in an exemplary fashion, was accepted and fainted from strain and relief.

The procedure for learning a role is a very personal matter, like getting to know the ways of a new wife or husband, and should be treated with as much affection. Maria Callas used to shut herself up with the score and remain alone until she had absorbed her stage character completely – with what result is already operatic history. Other singers prefer to take it upon themselves gradually, often with the assistance of others. But it is necessary to find a means of close identification through the score in order that the personality of the character and the personality of the singer are merged and become one, without distortion of either. The sooner this is accomplished, the easier it will be to learn the role, for it falls into place easily and naturally.

At this point the opera conductor may wish to take the singer through the role, either playing the piano himself, or leaving himself freer to direct the singer by letting one of his musical staff accompany. This will be an exciting, perhaps even a testing experience, although the 'safer' the character has become, musically and dramatically, the better the result will be. Then comes the first *Sitzprobe* or 'seated rehearsal' (a useful German word that has become wide adopted) with piano, as shown in the picture on page 62. Shortly after that, there will be a *Sitzprobe* with the cast sitting on chairs across the stage of the opera house, accompanied by the full orchestra in the pit. This is usually a very enjoyable and fairly relaxed experience because there are no costumes, movement or lights to think about, just the words and music – and scores are allowed.

Then comes the *Generalprobe* or dress rehearsal, when most peoples' nerves and faculties are wound up to the highest pitch. With full costume, make-up, scenery and lighting and everything as authentic as possible – even perhaps an invited audience – the singer's stage creation has got to be a real person, not merely a twentieth-century man or woman dressed up in somebody else's clothes.

And of course that is followed by all the excitement and glamour and publicity of the first night, with banks of flowers piled up in bouquets at the stage door, an atmosphere of tenseness and anticipation throughout the opera house where all the staff seem to be on the singer's side, wishing 'Good luck' to everybody who is to appear before the audience and those critics. Anybody who is an artist of even the most modest sort suffers from first-night nerves and it is no disgrace to do so; good training, good rehearsing and self-confidence overcome them after the first few minutes on stage and make the rest of the evening one of a challenge accepted, a task achieved – and the due amount of appreciation and applause.

Usually a first night will go without a hitch, but there have been several remarkable ones where the *prima donna* has thrown a fit of temperament and walked off after the first act, making it necessary to find another at this minimum notice and ensure that the two are kept as far apart as possible while changing over. For fisticuffs between *prime donne* are not to be ruled out. Indeed, Mozart wrote an opera on this subject called *The Impresario* in which the impresario has to sort out two of them who are squabbling about which will get one part. Impresarios are usually canny enough to be able to deal with these ladies, even inviting a rival to the first night in anticipation of an 'accident' after the first act.

In 1938, Lotte Lehmann was singing at Covent Garden in the summer season and was most concerned about her jewelry which was being smuggled out of Austria for her. Since she was not a Nazi (and had never been one) some members of the company made life extremely difficult for her, for they were either party members or fellow travellers. On account of this treatment, and for the first time in her career, she was unable to continue in her famous portrayal of the Marschallin in *Der Rosenkavalier* beyond the levée scene, and the curtain came down. The performance continued after a long interval when Hilde Konetzni, who had been in the audience, took over from the place where Mme Lehmann had stopped. She recovered and resumed a day or two later.

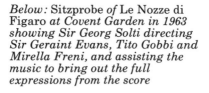

Below: Sitzprobe *of* Le Nozze di Figaro *at Covent Garden in 1963 showing Sir Georg Solti directing Sir Geraint Evans, Tito Gobbi and Mirella Freni, and assisting the music to bring out the full expressions from the score*

Lotte Lehmann (b. 1888) in her most famous role as the Marschallin, Marie Thérèse in Der Rosenkavalier, *which she sang for the first time at Covent Garden in 1924 and created a new standard of characterisation and lyrical interpretation*

The next 'performance' by Mme Lehmann in London was in 1957 when she coached singers in individual scenes from operas at public classes. Although she no longer sang, Mme Lehmann gave powerful demonstrations of Leonore (*Fidelio*), Zerbinetta and Ariadne and the Marschallin, among others, merely by speaking the text to a piano accompaniment. But it was the expressions on her face, the way she moved, how she held her hands, beside the finesse of diction and sheer identification with her characters that made it such a moving experience. Nobody in those audiences could have been convinced that they had not heard Mme Lehmann actually *singing*. And there were many singers in those audiences, watching and learning from the great singing-actress of the inter-war years.

Mme Lehmann expressed the most marvellous feeling of generosity towards her colleagues and pupils, which is the hallmark of a great singer. Yet even if two artists hate each other, there is usually a standard of decorum that is upheld. One celebrated tenor was even more celebrated by his colleagues for his bad breath: to play a love scene with him was torture. Another, a baritone this time, was given to spitting hard upon the stage – or on the feet of any other singer within range – to clear his throat for the next 'long sing'.

Occasionally a singer actually gives up his part in a performance to another, but there has to be a remarkably good reason. When the Vienna State Opera visited Covent Garden in 1947, that great tenor Richard Tauber had been a refugee in London since 1938, unemployed by either opera company and still in fine voice. He and Elisabeth Schumann (also living in London) were in the audience on the first night of the Vienna Opera season and Tauber was able to meet his old friends after nearly ten years' separation from them. It was suggested that he should sing one performance of Ottavio in *Don Giovanni*, and the tenor cast for it, Anton Dermota, earned everlasting gratitude by generously stepping down and allowing his peerless predecessor in the role to be heard once again, and for the last time. For Tauber was already dying and on the morning after his magnificent performance he was taken to a nursing home, never to leave there alive.

Dermota was, some years after that, the subject of a prank in Vienna because his colleagues considered that he was being too greedy. He was due to sing – as usual – the short role of Narraboth in Strauss's *Salome* one evening, and had arranged a *Lieder* recital for himself at a concert hall not far away, to start after his participation in the opera was over. Narraboth commits suicide and is carried off, and, having sung the part many times before, Dermota was quite certain that he had plenty of time to change and reappear before another audience. The whole cast of *Salome* knew about this, in fact Dermota had impressed upon them the fact that he was going to be paid twice over for an evening's work. So the cast formed a plan.

The curtain went up with the clarinet *glissando* from the pit which begins the work, and Dermota, in good voice, sang 'Wie schön ist die Prinzessin Salome heute Nacht!' He went through the familiar moves and emotions, was unable to restrain Salome from seeing Jokanaan, stabbed himself and fell dead on the stage. Herod, sung by Julius Patzak, entered, slipped in Narraboth's blood, showed fear at the ill-omen, asked who had ordered the young Syrian captain's death. Then he should have commanded his slaves to remove the body, but Patzak omitted the very words which Dermota had been waiting for: 'Fort mit ihm!' Time went on and he was still lying there, grunting and winking at anybody who came into view, for of course he could not move a muscle. Unfortunately none of the other singers seemed to notice that anything was wrong, and failed to respond. After about twenty minutes, and what seemed an eternity to Dermota, Patzak gave a flourish of the hand as a signal for the removal of

63

Salome (Strauss-Lachmann/
Wilde). Scene from the English
National Opera production of 1975.
Contrast this brooding Salome
(Josephine Barstow, downstage)
with Grace Bumbry's view of the
sulky girl on page 105. From left
to right: Emil Belcourt as Herod,
Terry Jenkins as 3rd. Jew, John
Winfield as 4th. Jew, Elizabeth
Connell as Herodias (on the
gallery), Stuart Kale as 1st. Jew
and John Tomlinson as 5th. Jew

the body. It is said that Dermota's much-advertised *Lieder* recital did not do him full justice.

As somebody once said, being an opera singer must be like always having an illness. The amount of careful dieting, rest before performances and non-availability at many social events through lessons or engagements puts a singer into the category of a convalescent. This is also true because of every singer's need to take remarkable care of herself. A certain way of catching a cold, laryngitis, bronchitis or even pneumonia is to stand outside the stage door in the winter, signing autographs immediately after emerging from the cosy warmth of the opera house. This is why the careful singer finds another way out of the house and is not being selfish or mean to her fans: she is protecting herself for future performances. Giovanni Martinelli's personal recipe was a warm, woolly scarf across the mouth, no talking, straight home and early to bed.

Not every singer will agree, however, especially as most are ravenously hungry afterwards. It does not do to eat before a performance, either for the voice or the digestion, but singing is a physical occupation, needing sustenance like any other exertion, which accounts for singers' apparently huge appetites in favourite restaurants late at night.

Wagnerian singers need ample fortification for their performances. Kirsten Flagstad used to lose several pounds in weight while singing Isolde, but found that Guinness was a fine pick-me-up during intervals. Lauritz Melchior, that apparently inexhaustible Tristan, used to find himself at a loose end in the first act, sitting behind the sail by the mast of the ship while waiting for his scene with Isolde to begin: either Flagstad, Frida Leider or Helen Traubel, as a rule. One evening before a performance in London he asked Beecham whether he might not creep on to the ship late, rather than sit there so long with nothing to do. Beecham said he would think of something, but asked the tenor to do as usual that night. He agreed to do so, and, much to his surprise and delight, when he took up his position he found a bottle of champagne and a glass there. The first part of *Tristan* Act I passed quicker than ever before. A number of years later in New York, Melchior ran into another Wagnerian *Heldentenor* (with whom he was on speaking terms) who said he was glad to see the Great Dane, and had he not sung Tristan at Covent Garden many times? Melchior replied that of course he had, but why the question? 'Well,' said the other man, 'when I took up my position behind the mast at the start of the opera – ' 'You found a bottle of champagne there', cut in Melchior. 'I know. That was my doing and it will go on. The champagne is in their prompt-book.'

Costume design for the Executioner in Salome

Occasionally, very occasionally, a singer will arrive in the opera house for a performance having dined too well. At the Vienna Opera under Clemens Krauss's regime, the bass-baritone singing Pizarro in *Fidelio* was determined to go on in spite of his parlous condition. This villainous character enters to dialogue, instructing the captain of the guard to double the sentries, or his head will fall, and then reads a letter. On the occasion in question, the dialogue was not only severely abridged, but consisted of mumbled words and waving of arms while the singer performed a series of unmilitary gyrations upon the stage. But when his crumbling speech gave way to the great aria 'Ha! welch ein Augenblick!' it was perfectly sung, admirably controlled and full of drama. Any member of that audience who had imagined that anything was wrong with the singer cleared his mind of such a misconception at once, and applauded vigorously – until the singer stood sideways, acknowledging the appreciation as if it was coming from the wings!

There are three things for a singer to beware of in the course of a performance, and the first is too much alcohol. The other two are related: animals and children. If they are included in the scenario and appear upon the stage, they are certain to rivet the attention of an audience, either with expectancy at what the animals might do, or else because the children 'look so sweet'. Sir Thomas Beecham's remark about the horse that misbehaved grossly during a performance of *Götterdämmerung* was 'Ah! Performer *and* Critic!' Such an event is invariably greeted with mirth nearly as much as when a (presumably different) horse rears up on its hind legs in an effort to unseat its singing rider.

Children are cast in several operas – *Hänsel und Gretel, La Bohème, Carmen* – for show and pleasant enjoyment. The children in *Peter Grimes, Turn of the*

Below left: Informal picture taken in Venice and showing Benjamin Britten, John Piper, his wife Mifanwy and their children, and Basil Coleman, picnic-ing in a small square behind the opera house two days before the première there of the Britten–Henry James opera, The Turn of the Screw, *in 1954*

Below: Turn of the Screw. *Jennifer Vyvyan as the Governess and David Hemmings as the malign child in a tense scene from the opera*

Below right: Don Carlos. *Revival in 1958 at Covent Garden showing Boris Christoff as King Philip II being temporarily put to silence while his wife Elisabetta bids farewell to her faulty chaperone who has just been banished by the King. All eyes are on the dogs during the aria*

Screw and *Wozzeck* are seen in entirely different, unnerving situations, which heighten the drama and make them the subject of horror or pity to an audience. As this is often beyond the power of adult artists, one can understand a singer's maxim, 'never appear in the same scene as animals or children'. In the picture below, Boris Christoff looks as if he wished he had remembered it.

Children's singing voices, as soloists, need great care in placing on the stage if they are to be heard properly. The shepherd boy in *Tosca* is not seen and has to project from behind the backcloth; the three boys in *Zauberflöte* are more safely cast as women although Glyndebourne has used three choristers from Canterbury with excellent effect; and if the solo voice from on high in *Parsifal* is a boy, it achieves that extra ounce of effect that Wagner probably intended.

Apart from principals, soloists, supporting singers, children and animals, there is another ingredient in an opera: the chorus. In the smaller German opera houses this stalwart body is composed of locals who are not, strictly speaking, professionals although they help the finances of their opera by occupying this useful and enjoyable job on a part-time basis. Otherwise the chorus is on the payroll of the opera house where it is administered and trained by its resident chorus-master. Members of the chorus know a great number of operas in several languages but are not inclined towards outstanding histrionic ability. As one of them said: 'It's all the same to us. We know what the opera is by the clothes put out for us to wear. Then we carry on as usual.'

The question as to whether it is possible to graduate from the chorus to solo roles must bear the answer 'Yes', for it has been done. The chance may or may not come quickly. David Ward began in Sadler's Wells Chorus, Peter Pears in Glyndebourne's, which shows that ability will not be put down.

Above: The Trojans. *Entry of the Horse into Troy. Production by Sir John Gielgud, sets and costumes by Mariano Andreu. Covent Garden 1957*

Right: Stage of the Drottningholm Theatre showing grooves for the scenery

Opposite: Fidelio. *Design by Hainer Hill for the prison scene in Act I showing the cells on the left, the jailer's house on the right and a small patch of (very significant) sky. Covent Garden 1961*

IV The Great Illusion

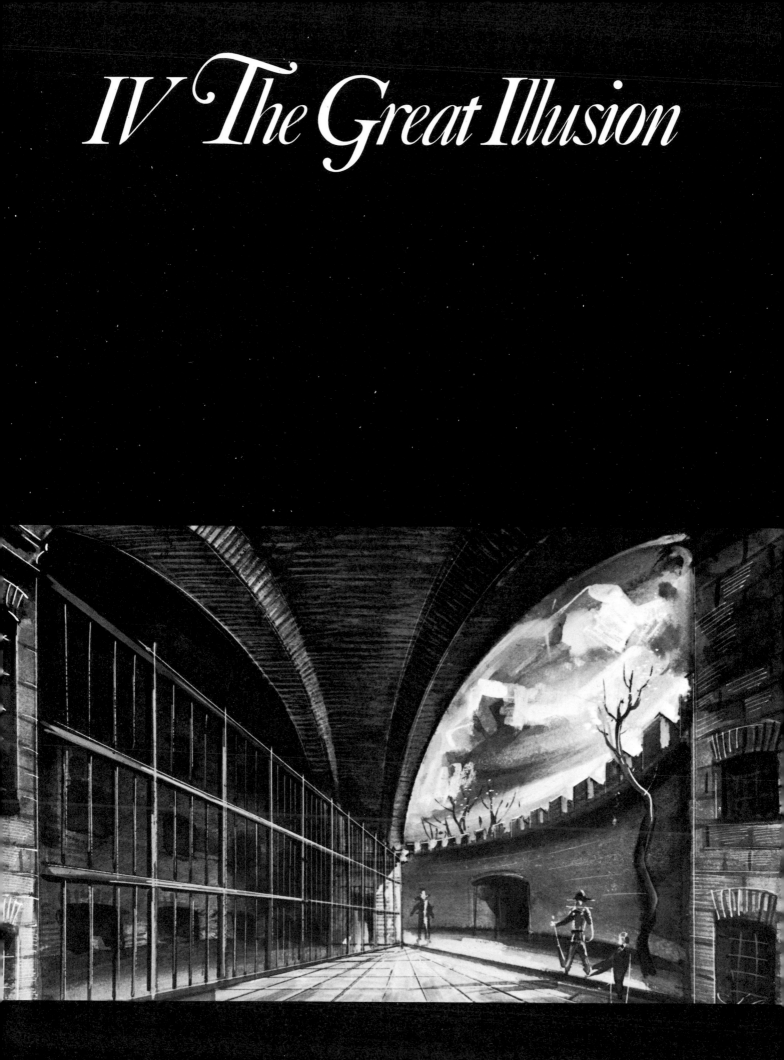

pera, of all the visual arts, is the most ritualistic. The vocal music is of prime importance, and all the rest must be as the setting to enhance this jewel. So far as the visual aspect is concerned, there is sometimes a great deal to be done by the designer to offset the *fait accompli* of large-scale mortals who by no means visually fit the roles in which they have been cast – vocally cast.

Because of this compensating necessity, scenery occupies a special place on the opera stage. It must go further than the scenery for a play, which need denote only a place and precious little else. An opera set has to underline the mood, even project it. Scenery can dwarf the singers or it can help accentuate their importance in the picture. Projected scenery of enormous buildings or built scenery of – say – the underside of the Trojan Horse in Berlioz's *La Prise de Troie*, puts the audience in the larger scale, when they see the singers as Lilliputians because the scenery is *vertical*. By reducing the scale of the scenery, as in *Das Rheingold*, and by the positions of the two giants, Fasolt and Fafner, horizontal lines accentuate these characters in size and have the effect of diminishing the gods.

At the beginning of the age of opera it was taken for granted that the scene would be magnificent to look upon and the singers clothed gorgeously, for the opera had developed directly from the Italian theatre of the seventeenth century. In the earliest operas, all scenery was two-dimensional. 'Flats' moved in grooves parallel to the audience for scene changes, and in front of a painted cloth at the back of the stage. The pretty little theatre at Drottningholm near Stockholm still preserves this system intact. Lighting was by candles, and the illusion of bulk and perspective was achieved by the designers' skill. (See picture on page 68.) Only with the advent of gas lighting, then of electricity, did the whole science of stage illusion and presentation become changed, controlled and more or less as we expect it today.

Such was the expectation of the audience in the seventeenth and eighteenth centuries that, as well as the best voices and excellent tunes in their operas, they demanded a vivid scene and rich costumes. Opera is considered to be a lavish entertainment, and so anybody who dislikes *Fidelio* simply because it takes place in a prison is merely echoing the words of the pompous major-domo of an ignorant master in *Ariadne auf Naxos*. He complains (in Hofmannsthal's words) because the scenery for the opera being presented 'before the richest man in Vienna' is only a desert island.

In a well co-ordinated production the scenery should be suitable to the occasion. The more glorious the occasion, like *Aida*, *Don Carlos*, *Semiramide* or *Turandot*, the more splendid must be the scene. But as we come forward to the psychological operatic dramas of the present day, *The Ledge*, *Il Prigioniero*, even *Wozzeck*, the suitability of the scene must be restricted to the misery inherent in each story.

But the choice and the design of scenery and costumes is not a one-sided affair in which the artist goes ahead and does it all as he thinks best. The lead which his producer gives him and the direction which they must both take together is carefully explored as a team effort in which the conductor plays a large part. The planning which goes into a production, well before it ever reaches rehearsal stage, perhaps as much as three years before, is long and arduous. At that long distance it may seem far removed from the eventual delights which meet the eye on the first night.

One of the most celebrated of Austrian stage designers, Alfred Roller, was resident designer at the Royal Vienna Opera from 1903 to 1909 under the great Gustav Mahler. He designed *Der Rosenkavalier* for Strauss and Hofmannsthal in Dresden in 1911, and played an important part on the visual side when the

Opposite left: Two silk programmes issued to box-holders from the middle of the last century. Their edges have been sewn down to prevent fraying but the gold cord on the blue programme is original

Opposite right: Silk programme from a State occasion at Covent Garden when King George V and Queen Mary entertained the King and Queen of Denmark shortly before the First World War

Rolling up a 'masking curtain' as seen from the fly floor of an opera house

Inset: Adjusting an arc lamp. Positive and negative carbon sticks have to be kept trimmed as they slowly burn away while causing a brilliant white spark between them, end to end. This light is projected on to the stage as a beam

Opposite above: Auditorium of La Scala, Milan, built in 1778, bombed in 1943 and reopened in 1946

Opposite below: Interior of the new Metropolitan Opera House, New York, in the Lincoln Center

Three illustrations from the 1951 re-opening Festival Ring *at Bayreuth, more formal than in 1976:*
Top: Siegfried *Act III. Siegfried (Bernd Aldenhoff) awakes the sleeping Brünnhilde (Astrid Varnay)*
Centre: Götterdämmerung. *The Oath Duet Act II. Siegfried (Aldenhoff) and Brünnhilde (Varnay) both swear contradictory vows on Hagen's (Ludwig Weber's) Spear. Gutrune (Martha Mödl) and the Vassals look on in horror*
Bottom: Die Walküre *Act II. Wotan (Sigurd Björling) and Brünnhilde (Astrid Varnay) meet in a rocky pass. This particular set, in its effectiveness, was an exception to the rest of the* Ring *setting*

Salzburg Festivals began. At the first one to include operas, in 1922, Roller designed *Don Giovanni*, *Nozze di Figaro*, *Così fan Tutte* and *Entführung*.

Many of the details for his *Rosenkavalier* enterprise have been recorded in the Strauss-Hofmannsthal correspondence, while all his drawings, in colour, for about 100 costumes and the three act sets are published as reproductions. The skill of the artist is remarkable, his imagination is extensive.

German opera has generally been more adventurous and advanced in method than that of any other part of the Western world, especially since the use of electric light on the stage. German provincial opera houses were the most advanced in technical equipment and stage machinery until their destruction during the last war, although the trend has now gone away from an excess of supporting mechanics in the theatre in general. If the adage that it is the singer who makes the opera is to be believed, this must be the reason.

Frankfurt was the first opera house in which a revolving stage was installed, in 1896, after which refinements in other German houses included provision for the whole stage to sink into the bowels of the house, for it to be moved to one side, and for another stage to be hoisted up in view of the audience, containing

Das Rheingold *at Bayreuth 1952. The characters are: left, Loge; Froh and Donner up centre; Wotan centre-stage; Freia and Fricka right*

a different set. Beside this, the meagre devices incorporated in the old opera houses which still stand are certainly compensated for by the accumulated atmosphere which has remained. Who, for instance, would not still prefer the old 'Diamond Horseshoe' in New York? Who would like to see a 'new' Covent Garden? But there are plans for better stage facilities in London.

Despite the destruction of many great opera houses in the last war, the Vienna State Opera, the Oper unter den Linden in Berlin, the Munich State Opera and Semper's Opera House in Dresden, to name the most prominent, one remained untouched. This was Wagner's Festspielhaus at Bayreuth, opened in 1876 and built especially to accommodate *Der Ring*. A few years later, at the turn of the century, the German-Swiss 'prophet' of the theatre, Adolph Appia, was concentrating his thoughts and efforts so as to improve the impact of scenery, mainly by following Wagner's demands that are fully set out in his scores and elsewhere. Appia was unable to understand how Wagner, with his complete grasp of the *Gesamtkunstwerk*, could remain satisfied with his two-dimensional scenery when, after all, scenery has three-dimensional singers to support.

There were several disciples of Appia, who strove to put his theories into practice; fashions in stage design came and went, but it was Max Reinhardt who, in the inter-war years, made his mark in quite a different way. Not until 1951 were Appia's ideals brought to fruition by the grandsons of Richard Wagner, Wieland and Wolfgang, and at Bayreuth too. Their production of *Der Ring* shocked and disgusted the diehards who felt that the Cycle is the most romantic expression and should be treated accordingly. Instead of three gorgeous Rhinemaidens swimming about in a well-lit 'river' at the opening of *Das Rheingold*, we saw, just after 4 p.m. on that sunny July afternoon, a completely dark stage. After a few moments of peering, three white dots became discernible in the blackness, and these turned out to be the faces of Elisabeth Schwarzkopf and two other singers which moved about a little (but only a little). How far they moved or where was impossible to judge because nothing else could be seen at all. This spare realisation ill accorded with all Wagner's precise stage directions in the score and integrated with the score; instead it employed cultivated darkness in which was tightly controlled light. Wagner's verisimilitude was thrown away, and practically all properties, certainly all the animals, were dispensed with.

But eventually some general light came up and what we saw as the basis of the set – and it remained throughout the Cycle – was an 'upturned saucer'. It occupied the whole of the acting area in an architectural manner, and the picture on page 77 shows how it was used. It allowed the maximum flexibility of movement as well as being of ideal shape and texture to accept light. Light was used like paint, to illuminate and to colour the scene in great swathes, and the one great advantage lay in rapid scene changes that carried through the sweep of the story: for scene changes in the 1951 *Ring* meant *mood* changes, all done by lighting. It was so subtle that one performance was too short a time to grasp the skill and daring with which this new presentation had been conceived. Furthermore, the timelessness of the story was further enhanced.

From then on, all forward-looking opera managements mounted similar kinds of Ring production on variants of the upturned saucer, including a sort of 'ring' like a saucer with the middle omitted. Since the upstage part of it was higher than the rest, this gave way to the idea of the *tilted* saucer, and so on. Twenty-five years later there seemed a need for fresh thinking, and the Bayreuth centenary year of 1976 certainly got it in a 'Victorian' production by Patrice Chéreau, conducted by Pierre Boulez, and for the next six years.

The *Ring* is certainly a timeless story, but opera economics press harder from one season to the next, so it seems unlikely that we shall ever again encounter those glorious sights such as Fricka's rams, really swimming Rhinemaidens, Brünnhilde actually riding her horse Grane into the flames of Siegfried's funeral pyre at the end of *Götterdämmerung* before the Hall of the Gibichungs comes crashing down in an avalanche of columns and a splintered roof. Even so – and here the Wagner brothers knew exactly what they were doing – so much of this colour and visual description is already in the score.

To make Siegfried go through each stage of forging his sword 'Nothung' might seem an unnecessary dotting and crossing in swordsmith's terms, because we can hear it all going on in the orchestra. All the same it is a most exciting moment in the third opera, *Siegfried*, prefacing the hero's destruction of the dragon, Fafner. Before 1951 this sword-forging business had its hazards, and one disastrous performance must have chalked up nearly every possible accident in terms of stagecraft. When the electrician in charge of working the sizzles and flashes and puffs of smoke in Mime's smithy got out of phase with

Siegfried *Act I. Siegfried (Wolfgang Windgassen) cleaves the anvil with his newly-forged sword 'Nothung'. Mime, the evil dwarf, cannot bear to see his protegé's success*

the action, astonishing displays of fireworks happened at the places about the stage where Siegfried was not at that moment standing. Finally the singer had great difficulty in working the foot pedal which caused the anvil to fall in two pieces. It needed a *double* stroke of 'Nothung' to produce the effect, coupled with an unexpected display of brisk footwork. But that was not all. When Siegfried encountered Wotan in the last act, the god's spear unaccountably broke in half some twenty minutes before Siegfried hacked at it with the same sword that had (eventually) shattered the anvil. Entirely composed, the singer (Hans Hotter) picked up a reserve spear and restored Wotan's power and dignity. This spear was broken properly at the right moment later on, but by now the audience was greatly puzzled as to what might – or might not – be happening next.

Transparencies, and scenes which change before one's eyes in the manner of a Victorian pantomime, are simply achieved. In operatic terms they are best described by Wagner, and these are his requirements between the end of the first scene and the beginning of the second in *Das Rheingold* – an opera which takes 2¾ hours, is in four scenes, and is played without interval or a break in the music:

> With terrible strength Alberich tears the gold from the rock and then scrambles hastily down, where he quickly disappears. Thick darkness falls suddenly as the Rhinemaidens dive down after the robber. *The river falls with them into the depths below. All the rocks disappear in thickest darkness as the whole stage, from top to bottom, is filled with black billows of water which, for some time, appear continuously to sink. Gradually the waves give place to clouds which, as light of increasing brightness is seen behind them, clear in the form of fine mist.* When these mists have been entirely dispersed in the form of faint cloudlets, an open space on a mountain becomes visible in the dawning light of early morning. Wotan, and near him Fricka, both sleeping, lie at one side in a flowery meadow. The dawning day lights up with increasing lustre a castle with glittering turrets, standing on a rocky brow at the back; between this and the foreground is supposed to be a deep valley through which the river Rhine flows.

That part of the scene printed in italic type is achieved on the stage by throwing moving pictures on to a gauze curtain while the scenery is being physically changed behind it. In practical terms, the audience's attention is engaged throughout the change and the drama's tension is retained by these visual 'effects'.

A land of make-believe, the 'Eastern Isles' is the setting for the Hofmannsthal–Strauss opera *Die Frau ohne Schatten* ('The Woman without a Shadow'). The work is infused with adult problems among the striving forces of good and evil in the manner of *The Magic Flute*. The picture on page 81 shows a setting by the Czech designer, Josef Swoboda, which makes great use of projected scenery, that is to say a kind of picture thrown as it were from a magic lantern, sufficiently powerfully to make it look solid. The huge 'flowers' dissolve when the scene changes, or rather melts before the eyes into something else. By this method (not new in the history of scenery by any means) many awkward scene changes can be effected instantly, at the touch of a switch, enhancing the sweep of the action and the impetus of the act. It is of great assistance and delight to the producer too.

Collaboration between conductor, producer and designer is essential if an opera production is to achieve full integrity through the orchestra, voices and beyond. It is the sound which motivates all movement upon the stage, for once the curtain has gone up it cannot come down again (barring accidents) until that place in the score marked 'Slow Curtain' or 'Fast Curtain'. In between are what the musicians describe as 'lots of dots'. All changes must be done promptly on cue, as the composer has regulated them, and like the beginning of *Das Rheingold*, already noted, the music confines the time allowed.

'The most romantic of German operas', *Der Freischütz*, produced over half a century before *Der Ring*, is a darker and more magic story than *Die Meistersinger*, to which it is similar in outline. Both operas have heroes determined to

Franco Zeffirelli's set for Falstaff *Act I Scene i, the Garter Inn, showing the table and balcony (right) with which Pistol and Bardolph performed their gymnastics. The steps proved vehicles down which Mistress Quickly approached with her 'Reverenza', in Act II Scene i*

win their brides through a competition. In *Der Freischütz* the hero, Max, consorts with evil forces to do so, and the most gripping part of the opera, scenically, is in the haunted Wolf's Glen where he goes to obtain magic bullets from Samiel, the Devil's agent. Signs of the horrible rites that take place in the Wolf's Glen include skeletons, black magic paraphernalia, flying witches and flashes from the magic bullets as they are being made. There is scope for the scene to be really horrible, but more often it can cause amusement from audiences unable to appreciate the German romantic idiom.

By contrast, the Italian opera from Bellini and onwards seldom needs such advanced or complicated scenery as the German, but feeds off colour and spectacle. Old flats, enormous cloths (never mind the creases), a few rostrums and steps for the singers' manoeuvres, an entirely new (or rather *different*) stage picture for each act, and as cavernous a stage as possible are the modest demands. The stage needs to be large in case the ballet comes along and performs too, as it does in *Aida*, *La Gioconda*, *William Tell*, and all the Meyerbeer operas because they emanated from Paris. It may look amateurish sometimes, and it is not what the art of opera is all about.

For the Italians (and to an equal degree the Viennese) go to hear the singing. Their prime consideration is to have every note in its place, so if this is the case while the scenery and costumes are a visual jumble – never mind! This does not mean that the most celebrated designers are not employed for Italian operas,

because they most certainly are, although great names do not necessarily produce great results. 'Cecil Beaton's *Turandot*' to put it the way the Press always does, was exactly that, and some distance from Puccini's *Turandot*.

The Italian producer and designer, Franco Zeffirelli, on the other hand, has been extremely successful, for he is a real man-of-the-theatre. His sets for *Tosca*, created for Callas and Gobbi at Covent Garden, and then lent to the Paris Opéra for performances with the same singers, were an admirable realisation, especially for singers of such quality. The solidity and authentic appearance of the scene, down to the last detail, were perhaps an indication of the way in which Italian opera is now going, compared with German design. In other words, they appear to have crossed over.

Today the Italians still prefer pageant and colour, but with more substance, like the services in the Roman Catholic Church. The Germans favour more Lutheran – if not Presbyterian – austerity in their design, where the sign 'Repent ye, Sinner!' is implicit, if not exactly visible.

Zeffirelli also designed and produced an excellent *Falstaff* (the set design is shown above) and it maintained an utterly naturalistic aspect until the last act when, lo and behold, the scenery of Windsor Forest all flew away in view of the audience to reveal an almost bare stage for the finale. This seems a mixture of styles: perhaps best avoided when one has endeavoured to give a total illusion up to the last moment.

Douglas Robinson, Chorus Master at Covent Garden from 1945–72, takes his cue for the off-stage chorus from a closed-circuit television which relays the conductor's beat immediately from the pit, out of view backstage

One might, indeed, be forgiven for having thought something had gone seriously wrong on the stage, as actually did happen during a routine performance of *Il Trovatore* in English. In the first scene, an old man, Ferrando, is telling the audience (via some stage soldiers) what has happened in the story many years before the opera has begun. After his history lesson, a little portcullis in an archway of the castle courtyard was meant to rise so as to admit the Count de Luna. But on Ferrando's words: 'Bestir ye! Bestir ye!' the whole back wall of the castle vanished from sight, leaving unlikely bits and pieces in full view. When the wall returned, somewhat shyly, they got on with the opera.

Strangely enough, much the same sort of thing happens in another scene of *Il Trovatore* – the Miserere Scene – during the Marx Brothers film *A Night at the Opera*, when backcloths go up and down in an alarming manner. The most unexpected one to come to rest for a few moments behind the fifteenth-century pair of lovers was the deck and superstructure of a US Navy battleship.

Singers are left absolutely defenceless when this sort of thing happens – although the Marx Brothers farce took the situation beyond normal possibilities. Yet what can really upset a singer on the stage is the absence of a prop(erty). A story is told of a Canadian soprano who was singing Manon in Massenet's opera. Having bid farewell to her little table in the second act, she has to ring a bell to summon her maid to send a letter of explanation as to why she is leaving Des Grieux. The bell had not been put on the table for her. So instead of calling for the maid, or signalling with her hand, she trilled 'Ting-a-ling-a-ling!'

Certain forms of costume, especially historic costume, have proved to be unsatisfactory upon the stage – whether in 'straight' theatre or operatic – and one of these is the dress worn by Cavaliers and Roundheads during the English

Civil War in the seventeenth century. There seems no reasonable explanation for this, but any male singer who has appeared in, for instance, *I Puritani*, will agree that he was in danger of causing unwonted laughs, especially if his dress was historically accurate. Perhaps the invading force of mockery and parody from television has something to do with it.

Yet even with a properly co-ordinated costume plan, a designer's efforts can still go wrong when a singer insists upon using (generally) *her* own costume, come what may. 'It's so much more comfortable than that thing they've given me to wear, dee-ar', she purrs at the designer, apparently oblivious of the fact that he created 'that thing' for her. This kind of attitude is occasionally met with today, and exaggerates the traditional image of the *prima donna*, whose interests seem seldom to stray far beyond herself.

In the whole production schedule, where a strict account is maintained of what has to be ready and when, there is generally a need for costume props quite early. These are items of dress and of requirements during the plot (like Manon's bell) which are necessary during rehearsals. Very early on there will be substitutes, but nearer the time of the first night it is much better if the actual canes, cups, knives, swords and so on are really there to use. Their feel and familiarity are desirable to the singer. In the picture on page 94, the King of Egypt has a staff, but no other indication of who he is. This singer found the staff helpful with which to balance himself on those rather worn steps, as well as a useful aid to assert himself at this particular rehearsal.

Tosca wears a huge hat, dripping with ostrich feathers, and this must be worn in early rehearsals so that she may avoid (or ensure) complete eclipse of the tenor during close-ups. The same applies exactly to Falstaff, especially at the end of Act II when he dresses up in his finery to call on Mistress Ford, and has to pass through a doorway together with 'Master Brook'.

The control of singers backstage during the performance is the responsibility of the musical assistants as well as the stage management. A *prima donna* will usually require an escort from her dressing-room on to the stage where she is to make her entrance. She may even need 'putting on' at the correct moment to give her complete confidence, then fetching from where she makes her exit, and escorting her back to her dressing-room again. Musical assistants are found playing the piano at coaching sessions and rehearsals; conducting off-stage bands and choruses; being in charge of off-stage soloists and 'effects', but always musical 'effects'. In the old days before closed-circuit television was used to relay the conductor's beat visually to any part of the opera house, scenery sometimes got in the way with a vengeance. In order to convey the exact beat from the pit to a band far back, or to voices far up in the flies for some special effect as in *Parsifal*, there might be as many as three 'linkmen', one with his eye to a draughty hole in the scenery watching the conductor and cursing every time one of the singers moved across his line of sight. At the appropriate moment, yet allowing for the slight delay involved, he would wave to the next man behind him – without looking at anyone but the conductor – and No. 2 would wave in turn to the repetiteur or whoever was conducting in the distance. Sometimes the third man was needed if there were awkward corners in the scenery or the distance was great that had to be covered in terms of yards in a dimly lit area at the back of a dusty stage. For especially in the recesses of large stages it is impossible to hear either orchestra or singers.

The author recalls, in the days when he was learning his repertoire, being backstage during a performance of an old-fashioned production of *Das Rheingold*. He was standing in the downstage corner on the opposite prompt side, and above him sat an electrician with a 'magic lantern' ready to throw the picture of Valhalla on to the cyclorama when he got the cue towards the end

of the opera. As the time came nearer and Donner was 'Heda! Hedoing' away, the electrician called out for help, using no words that are in Wagner's libretto. The author, in no position of authority, nevertheless held the score of the opera, and for want of the presence of a musical assistant, he went through the procedure of telling the electrician to 'Stand by!', raised his hand, and dropped it as he hissed 'Go!' on 'Weise der Brücke den WEG!' Wotan had already started his concluding monologue 'Abendlich strahlt' when the musical assistant came running round, but by then the singers would have been enthusing about nothing visible if. . . .

Puccini's *Tosca* needs a good deal of help from musical assistants in the course of the action: Tosca's voice is first heard offstage; Scarpia needs to make his first entrance to split-second timing; Tosca's cantata in Act II is sung offstage with chorus; Cavaradossi's torture scene is out of sight of the audience, but sometimes there are intentionally visible shadows, and all has to be carefully cued in; and the shepherd boy's song offstage at the start of Act III, accompanied by bells, has to be precisely dovetailed with the orchestra in the pit.

One member of the musical staff faces the singers throughout the performance from the prompter's box in the footlights of many opera houses. He (usually, not she) is of enormous help to the singers by giving ('throwing' more often) their words to them a phrase in advance, so that they are hearing what they are going to be singing immediately afterwards. In such a complex ensemble as the fugue at the end of *Falstaff*, the prompter is invaluable and can even help to prevent an accident which might affect everybody.

Very occasionally a prompter will be lying concealed on the stage, inside or underneath part of the scenery or furnishings, when it is absolutely essential for the singer or singers to be able to hear him. This has the added advantage, especially when the performance is broadcast, of muffling the prompter's voice that can otherwise greatly detract from the singing with its endless interruptions.

Musical assistants are highly qualified musicians, on the way to becoming operatic conductors, producers or administrators in their own right. Sir Georg Solti was a young musical assistant to Toscanini at Salzburg in 1937; while at Bayreuth in 1892, three of the eight assistants were Siegfried Wagner, Max von Schillings (later the Director of the Berlin State Opera) and Engelbert Humperdinck (composer of *Hänsel und Gretel*).

Television opera has been attempted, with various success, since the early 1950s, not only as special studio productions, but as filmed live performances. The chief fault was the total disregard by the television directors of the fact that in the opera house there is no such thing as a close-up, because of the orchestra pit! The altogether unrealistic view down singers' throats to a well-formed uvula is seldom an interesting sight, even to doctors, but this style of television production continued remorselessly until *Owen Wingrave*.

This opera, specially written for television by Benjamin Britten, was later transferred (with moderate success) to the stage, but its original intentions, using only medium shots, were well carried out. The accent upon individual expressions, on groupings and whole bodies made a great change from seeing only parts of the face. Visually, as it turned out, it was too realistic to be operatic: the sets by David Myerscough-Jones were more theatrical, so that one could almost be forgiven for forgetting that it was an opera at all.

The television screen is far too small to encompass opera straight from the stage. All the camera can do is to bite off little pieces of the action in medium shot, or else to take it all in, when it is so small as to begin to lose all meaning. What a far cry this is from the opposite end of opera production: *Aida* or some such extravaganza at the Caracalla Baths or at the Verona Arena. The very

Flying Rhinemaidens in a traditional production of Das Rheingold *rehearsing their complicated movements in view of the audience, while miming singers' voices and emphasising their words by gestures*

Owen Wingrave (Britten–Piper). Britten's first opera for television in 1973. The angry Wingrave family, Sylvia Fisher, Peter Pears, Janet Baker and Jennifer Vyvyan being thoroughly disapproving of the pacifist Owen

Opposite: Another scene from the opera with Benjamin Luxon (seated) as Wingrave

magnitude of the scene forces the spectators to turn their heads from side to side so as to see everything that is going on. In one sense, the visual sense, opera is very glorious in such a setting. (See picture on pages 150–1.)

Opera in the cinema, even with the wide screen, is rather different, and has to be regarded as second best because it is one performance trapped, like a bee in amber, that can never change. The whole joy of going to the opera lies in the hope that *tonight* everything will go so well that it will be the best performance of that particular work *ever* to be heard at that opera house! The film of an opera, in contrast, is no more alive than an object in a museum compared with another in real life.

Even so, films of operas cannot be dismissed. Some moderately effective 'straight' films were made of Italian operas immediately after the last war, starring Tito Gobbi: *Rigoletto*, *La Forza del Destino* and *Pagliacci*. Each act began with the stage curtains being raised, and ended with their being lowered. The atmosphere of the opera house was thus quite well preserved and the scenes never went outside the stage. By contrast, Dr Paul Czinner filmed *Don Giovanni* and *Der Rosenkavalier* at Salzburg in performances which are already historical documents of stage production, design and musical styles of the time. These were made by mounting three or four cameras at entirely different places and letting them run for the whole performance. After a great deal of cutting the result achieved considerable variety and interest.

Later, Herbert von Karajan with his own film company has taken to making operatic films, combining them with performances at Salzburg Festivals and commercial recordings. To avoid extravagant facial expressions by the singers, they are filmed 'marking' their singing roles, and their real vocalisation is added on the soundtrack at a later stage.

There have been admirable Bolshoi films, especially a *Boris Godunov* by the Soviet director Stroyeva, using full cinematic resources of scenery and landscapes combined with restrained close-ups. By contrast, a German film of *Fidelio* descends to something approaching gimmickry by employing the music to the overture as a means of recording the arrival of a messenger on horseback over miles and miles of road, though admittedly through lovely scenery. The overture to an opera is intended to be listened to carefully, without distraction, for it will prepare the mind for what is to come.

In 1974 the Swedish director, Ingmar Bergman, was responsible for a film of *Die Zauberflöte*. It is sung in Swedish, some numbers are transposed, some are cut altogether, eccentric liberties are taken over casting and presentation, and the result, not only unoperatic, is decidedly un-Mozartean. One of the worst pieces of personal vanity occurs in the overture, almost guaranteed to put an intelligent and sensitive person off it for ever, and once again, it has little to do with the glory of opera. It merely makes use of Mozart's masterpiece as a vehicle – and a rickety vehicle at that – for a different medium.

V · The Voice from the Darkness

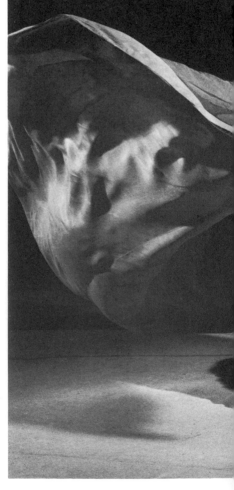

*I*t called out sharply from the darkness of the empty auditorium, telling the *prima donna*, in clipped phrases, that she had stepped out of the light and was now not only invisible but – with a pause as if of gratitude – inaudible. She shouted back into the void in broken English that she had never been so insulted in her life, and marched haughtily from the stage to see the Director. While she coaxed some real tears to add veracity to her story, the producer called for a short break, sighing at the waste of time but not bothering to follow the irate soprano or to concern himself with her any more.

She gained instant admission to the Director, who received her with a somewhat baleful expression and motioned her to a chair. She remained standing, stamped her foot and said 'I am singing my best woice when these *rüde* Mann say he no hear me, no want hear me. I am never taking this from a Englishmen.'

'Oh!' replied the Director. 'He isn't an Englishman, he's Irish.'

'Ahh!' she screamed, and gathering up her skirt, ran from the room, bounded down the stairs and on to the stage. She found the producer, wrapped her arms round his neck and kissed him. Although well accustomed to the unpredictable ways of highly volatile women, even he was surprised at this *volte face*. 'I am thinking you are Englishmen, darling,' she cooed at him. 'So is all right, yes? We go on where you stop me. So!' And she proceeded with the act, singing like an angel, keeping in the light and giving no more trouble.

This happened to Tyrone Guthrie at Covent Garden in the late 1940s. He was one example of a highly experienced theatrical producer who sometimes turned to opera. Although there are far more jobs going for producers in the theatre, especially in Britain, it is essential for them to possess a good grounding in the technique of straight plays before adapting their experience to the rigorous demands of the opera house. No matter how many interesting or original ideas a producer may have for a 'new' *Turandot*, a 'new' *Traviata* or 'an entirely revised and rethought production of . . .' whatever it may be, he is always and irrefutably bound by the score. Each and every bar of music contains him as if it were of iron. As we shall see, the producer can achieve modifications to suit the singers' needs, but always with the conductor's consent. The score binds every person working on the opera to the composer's intentions, and this is why so many drama producers consider themselves to be unduly inhibited in the opera house, and turn their backs upon it.

Ljuba Welitsch's dance of the seven veils in the 1949 Covent Garden production of Salome, *produced by Peter Brook and designed by Salvador Dali*

Others, in defiance of the composer and the score, have ridden roughshod over the musical framework, ignoring the concept that it must stand unchallenged and unmoved from beginning to end. Such occasions as these inevitably end in disaster, and on the way they cause an acknowledged drama producer to stamp the production with his name. How many times have we heard of So-and-So's *Figaro*; of Somebody-else's *Rigoletto*; or *Barber of Seville?* These three operas were composed, respectively, by Mozart, Verdi and Rossini, although from the publicity you would never think so. The producers seem to have made a thoroughly successful takeover bid.

So it was that the much-vaunted production of 'Peter Brook's *Salome*' at Covent Garden in 1949 caused one of the worst scandals in that house since Sir Thomas Beecham swore at a first night audience. Salvador Dali designed the scenery and costumes, Peter Brook, fresh from great successes at the Birmingham Repertory Theatre and Stratford-upon-Avon, produced, as he had recently been appointed resident producer of opera at Covent Garden. Karl Rankl, the musical director, disowned all but the music, to the extent of refusing to appear on the stage to take his call, or of speaking to Brook unless it was unavoidable. Salvador Dali never set foot in London, or else many of the absurdities in this, his first opera designs, would have been modified, at least. The singers, with one exception, were miserably unhappy in the costumes which Dali had designed for them, considering that he was generally trying to throttle them when he was not attempting to root them to the spot. The one exception, who was unconcerned because she was completely comfortable, was the star, Ljuba Welitsch, who wore her own Salome costume in defiance of Brook and the absent Dali.

The production was considered by all the critics and many of the audiences to be against the score, but when one recalls it after nearly thirty years it does not seem to have been any worse than a brave attempt at something new, far in advance of its time. Real artists have vision: Brook is a real artist. At the time he was a young and impetuous man who might have mellowed into granting the score a far more important place in his scheme of things; but he could not wait, and returned to the theatre with what accumulation of successes there we all know. Possibly the most unexpected turn to this strange production of *Salome* came after its eighth and last performance in December 1949 when the stage staff at the Royal Opera House, without waiting for instructions, smashed the set to pieces. They, too, had been infected with a hatred for it and took their revenge for the entire company against the designer and producer.

Another English stage producer and star actor who ventured into opera in 1958 was John Gielgud. He created a memorable production of Berlioz's grand two-part *Trojans*. Very few people who go to performances of this thrilling work can be unaware of the implications of the horse which the Greeks have persuaded the Trojans to drag inside their city. So here is a fine example of that ally to any producer: dramatic irony, where the audience is aware of the true situation in the story before the characters upon the stage realise it. (Sir) John Gielgud's horse was made to appear so enormous that, when it was wheeled on, all we could see was its four legs and under-belly!

Sir John has later stated that the producer of any spectacle (although he was chiefly concerned with plays) can greatly profit from being in it himself. After the agonies of the first night and subsequent press criticisms (which can, on occasions, wound sensitive people), certain modifications always become necessary as the production settles down. Some are so slight as to be imperceptible to an audience, others may be made more obvious by later developments which crop up. But if the producer is actually in the production, he recognises at once the need for fining down at the corners, and may even take part in them himself.

A morning rehearsal for an opera at Her Majesty's Theatre, London, in 1863

Imagine, therefore, the disgust of the producer who does not see his work after the first night until the following season. It may well have become degraded, in his opinion, and he will be furious about it. In the opera house, the cast may also have changed, and there will be different singers in important roles who have been coached in their moves by the resident producer or even by the stage manager. Since the original moves were made for these singers' rivals, they may not too readily accept them, and the human element now contributes towards disappointing the producer. And when the production, which was tailor-made for the first stage upon which it was heard, goes on tour – well, anything can happen. Smaller stages, larger stages, fatter or thinner stages all call for extensive modification in the singers' movements to and fro across the stage.

As a rule, the only man who is bound to be in an executive position for each and every performance is the conductor. Some conductors have fancied themselves as producers, very few have had anything like comparable talent on the stage to what they possess in the pit. Sir Thomas Beecham seldom interfered on the stage unless the situation demanded it, but on one occasion he did so to everybody's advantage. A scene change in Rimsky-Korsakov's *Le Coq d'Or* was taking far too long at final rehearsals. The highly experienced and redoubtable stage manager, Mr Ballard, was unable to improve matters until Sir Thomas intervened. The suggestions which came from the pit were received with caution, but as Sir Thomas called out in his unmistakable accent: 'Bring the tower in *first*; then the wall and steps; then . . .' and so on. It worked. This was either because Sir Thomas recognised the right approach by the light of nature, or because he was proposing the only sequence which had not so far been adopted. Everyone was highly impressed as the golden-domed tower with its crooked minaret, the golden wall and steps and fanciful backcloth all moved smoothly into place night after night.

Le Coq d'Or (Rimsky-Korsakov–
Byelsky) at Covent Garden in 1954.
Sets by Loudon Sainthill,
production by Sir Robert
Helpmann. Howell Glynne as the
senile King Dodon

Scores of years of experience in the pit do not always enable a conductor to contribute more than a flash of inspiration now and again, except that he can possibly see the happenings on stage with a more detached eye and from the best possible vantage-point. But it depends upon how well he gets on with the producer. Under normal circumstances, the conductor works via the score to the orchestra and the singers, while the producer encourages the singers to act, to be in the right place at the right time and to look beautiful, handsome, frightening or hideous as the case may be. The conductor is not concerned with any more than the sounds they make, and this is not only quite enough for him to attend to, but the driving force of the whole opera. On the other hand, he is not going to get the best sounds out of his singers if they are not entirely comfortable and confident, and can devote at least 50 per cent of their attention to him. If the producer has done his job properly, they will be comfortable, and may even have forgotten all about him, so intently will they be gazing at the conductor and waiting for the next cue from him.

This is not to belittle the producer's part in the whole enterprise, for he is responsible for the visual picture and for the patterns which the singers make as they move from one part of the stage to the other. The designer has created suitable scenery, and has clothed the singers in a manner appropriate to the period and to the style of the opera's story. He has also given each of them colours which help to support whatever conflicts or attractions there might be between them. By placing the singers on the stage so that these colours in their costumes will best come across to the audience, by also placing them so that they can always see the conductor, and by making the moves natural and effective, he will have done a thoroughly good job for the singers. The rest is implicit in physical or lighting requirements in the plot, and will depend upon the stage's resources.

Thus the liaison between conductor, producer and designer must be firm, sympathetic and, if possible, extremely close. The fact that there are three of them can sometimes lead to two being against one. Before and during the last war in Munich, there was an ideal triumvirate in the Munich State Opera. Clemens Krauss was the conductor, Rudolf Hartmann the producer and Ludwig Sievert the designer. Each was a highly cultured person and thoroughly appreciated and understood the others' needs and requirements. It is to be regretted that nowadays there is not the same institution as three resident artists in these capacities, for invariably the most suitable designer is called in for each production.

Dress rehearsal of Aida *Act I at Covent Garden in 1936. The stage manager is standing in for Radamés (Lauri-Volpi) while the King and Amneris (Gertrud Wettergren) show willing in their street clothes*

A rehearsal for Schoenberg's Moses and Aron at Covent Garden in 1965. Here the conductor and producer (Peter Hall) are working as a team in a big chorus number

When we consider the talent that is assembled in an opera house for the production of a new opera, it is apparent how expensive such an enterprise is bound to be. There is the poet, the composer, the producer, the conductor and the designer. There may even also be the *dramaturg* (or resident literary expert) and a musical director who is not going to conduct this particular work. Each of them may be fighting the whole time for his own particular needs – or what he imagines them to be – and it is so difficult for the one man who is indisputably the judge and final arbiter of it all to see it in perspective. And this is the conductor.

It was probably Richard Wagner who first saw clearly what he called the

Gesamtkunstwerk – the combined artistic endeavour – which opera most certainly has got to be if it is to succeed. An opera has been likened to an air balloon. When everything seems to be working perfectly and the wind is in the most favourable direction, it still refuses to become airborne, but remains like a leaden weight on the ground, dull, lifeless and completely disappointing. But on another night, suddenly, almost unexpectedly, it takes to the air and floats up near to heaven, beautiful – wonderful – entrancing to all who behold it! Thus something more than sheer hard work and inspiration are necessary from all quarters, and probably this indefinable thing is the result of complete integration and 'giving' between them. This is the very heart of *Gesamtkunstwerk*, the total collaboration between sister arts until one unified art is arrived at: the art of the Opera. Nevertheless, this implies one man at the top, an artistic dictator, who finances, controls, directs, produces – all this on top of his own creation: words and music.

Richard Wagner was one of two prime operatic innovators of the nineteenth century. The other was Giuseppe Verdi. But in terms of all-round potential and capability, Wagner was the greater of the two and a genius. (That word is used with great care, too.) His interests lay in politics, in the theatre, in writing and in music. He wrote his own librettos (after long and meticulous research), he set them to music, he invented new instruments if he felt their need, he produced his operas and conducted them. And when the scale of his ideas surmounted the technical possibilities of any opera house in Europe, he raised the

95

funds so that a *Festspielhaus* (or 'festival playhouse') might be built to accommodate these operas, based upon the classical amphitheatre but covered in with *wood*, and (more or less) to his own design. In August 1876 Wagner's Festspielhaus opened at Bayreuth, in Bavaria, with Wagner's *Das Rheingold*, the first of the four operas comprising *Der Ring des Nibelungen* (The Ring of the Nibelungs). These operas, each of three acts except the first, which Wagner regarded as a *Vorabend* (a 'preliminary evening'), should be played upon four successive evenings. *Das Rheingold* has four scenes which follow each other without a break. The music is continuous for $2\frac{3}{4}$ hours. The cycle tells of the gradual failure and final destruction of the mythological Norse gods, led by Wotan, because they ceased to uphold their own high principles and resorted to meanness and trickery more associated with mortals. But the meanings and shades of meanings in *Der Ring* have been argued about ever since 1876 and are good for at least another century.

All Wagner's operas tend to be discursive: he was primarily a musician, secondly a political wrangler and thirdly a librettist. The wrangling which goes on in his operas tends to clog the action, although his arguments develop along fascinating lines, provided one can hear the words and understand them. His characters, whether gods, giants, dwarfs, a dragon, a woodbird, demi-goddesses or mere mortals, stand for a long time and talk to each other. This is part of the technique. For after some ten minutes of physical inaction, when somebody does move, the impact is very great. Hence Wotan's rages are enormous; the Nibelung dwarfs' cries are terrifying; the slaying of the dragon and the complementary assassination of Siegfried are cruel and exciting to the depth of the senses. Were the action to be 'souped up' as in a film where something has got to move all the time, it would not be possible to register heights of emotion with such an economy of forces.

The challenge which faces the producer who agrees to stage this huge cycle is a fearsome one. And its ending, when the massive climax that Wagner demands engulfs the principal characters upon the stage and the emotions of the audience too, cannot better be described than in a translation of Wagner's own stage directions to the finale of *Götterdämmerung*:

> [Brünnhilde] springs on to her horse's back and, preparing him to jump, urges him with one leap into the burning pyre. The fire blazes high up, filling the whole space in front of the Hall, which it seems about to devour . . . When the whole stage seems enveloped in flames, the glow is suddenly extinguished so that only a cloud of smoke remains, hovering over the background and lying on the horizon like a thick fog-bank. At the same time, the Rhine swells up mightily and spreads its waters over the pyre. On its waves swim the three Rhinemaidens who make for the pyre. Hagen . . . is terribly alarmed at the sight of [them] . . . He hastily discards his spear, shield and helmet and plunges into the flood. The three Rhinemaidens throw their arms round his neck and draw him down as they swim away. Flosshilde holds aloft in exultation the Ring which she has taken from him. A red glare breaks through the cloudbank on the horizon, increasing in brightness. By its light, the Rhinemaidens can be seen swimming in a circle and playing with the Ring on the waves of the Rhine, which has now sunk to its original level. From the remains of the half-burnt Hall, the men and women behold with awe and terror the rising glow in the heavens. When this has reached its utmost brilliance, all Valhalla appears in it, with the gods and heroes assembled there. Bright flames appear to spring up in the Hall of the gods and when they are completely enveloped in flames, the curtain falls.

This may well seem impossible to realise effectively on the stage, but up to 1951 it was managed, with varying degrees of success, all over the Western world. During the last war, Wagner's operas continued to be performed at Bayreuth, under Hitler's special patronage, until 1944. After the fall of Germany, the forces of occupation prevented their revival until 1951. In this year, three-quarters of a century since its institution, the Festspielhaus reopened with a restudied *Ring* cycle and *Parsifal*. Not many people were aware of the extent of this 'restudy'. Richard Wagner's grandsons, Wolfgang and Wieland, were

Left: A scene in the wardrobe department attending to wigs for the evening's performance

Below: Relaxing in the dressing room between acts

jointly in charge, and after a lifetime of experience as children and as actual assistants at the pre-war festivals, they had conceived the whole thing anew. Wolfgang was more the administrator, but Wieland was the inspired and revolutionary producer. Indeed the 1951 Bayreuth Festival began an operatic revolution in much the same way as *musique concrète* was another. Wieland Wagner achieved most of his effects by lighting, painting in black and white the sounds of his grandfather's orchestra and the human voices, backed up by the emotion of the audience. For those of us who were there, it took some getting used to and seemed at first to be a huge disappointment. Instead of three wholly visible Rhinemaidens, swooping and diving in 'the moving water, which restlessly streams from right to left' round a central rock occasionally touched by sunlight, we saw three little singing faces in solid, velvet darkness. Instead of the cataclysm at the end of *Götterdämmerung* later in the week, there was a muted collapse of a couple of token columns with lights flashing and a general sense of let-down, rather than of fall-down.

But whereas the first post-war Bayreuth *Ring* was not – perhaps could not be – the complete Wieland Wagner realisation, his interpretation of *Parsifal* that year was possibly never bettered. The stage at Bayreuth is forty-five metres deep and beyond the back wall is a kind of inset 'cupboard' a further twelve metres deep, which is sometimes used as a scenery store (or used to be) and gives out through doors to the open air behind the theatre. The first time the procession of Knights of the Grail approached the centre of the stage, they came from outside the back of the 'cupboard', through it, and on to the stage and then down to the front. The first indication of this procession was a very small, dim and far-away movement which was scarcely discernible as a human being at all. When it was seen to be a man, and there were many others behind him in a column, moving as from a very great distance, the effect was extraordinary. The timing to the music was so perfect, too, that all the Knights were assembled at exactly the right moment on the main stage for their necessary involvement in the action. This was a real production stroke. While few stages can possibly allow for such expansive movement, those which can should sometimes be put to the test, and the test is in invention, interpretation, control, rehearsal and eventual achievement. However many hours this scene took to bring to perfection were well worth the trouble because it must remain indelibly in the memories of those who witnessed it for the first time.

Wieland Wagner, who unfortunately died in 1966, sometimes stepped outside the confines of his family tradition – mainly for the Stuttgart Opera – and produced other composers' operas. Beethoven's *Fidelio* in his realisation was harsh and military, Strauss's *Salome* was perverse and, on one occasion, its performances came to an untimely end after only a few minutes. The role of Herod's monstrous step-daughter was sung by Anja Silja, who used frequently to divide her time between Stuttgart and Bayreuth. On this particular occasion she had driven up the Autobahn, arriving somewhat exhausted in Stuttgart for the performance. Wieland Wagner's idea was to portray Salome as a kind of spider in a cobweb, hovering over the stage at the beginning of the opera. Poor Miss Silja was too tired to hang on to the ropes of the 'cobweb' for long, and fell out of it. The performance came to a premature conclusion.

Although Strauss's and Wagner's operas are performed in Italy, frequently in Italian, the Germanic operatic style does not altogether meet the requirements and preferences of the land of *bel canto*. Verdi and Wagner were exact contemporaries, both worked in their own ways for opera in their own lands, but from entirely different directions, and they never met. Verdi lived longer than Wagner, and by the end he, too, was tending to write less in separate arias and ensembles, than in whole, integrated scenes and acts. Here the similarity

98

Right: Boris Godunov
(Moussorgsky). Robert Tear as the
Simpleton surrounded by children,
in the Covent Garden production

Below: Ramón Vinay, the world's
reigning Otello between 1944–59,
seen making up for the role which
he first sang under Toscanini's
baton. Having begun his career as
a baritone, he reverted to the lower
voice and ended his short, but
brilliant career by singing Iago in
his native city of Santiago, in 1969

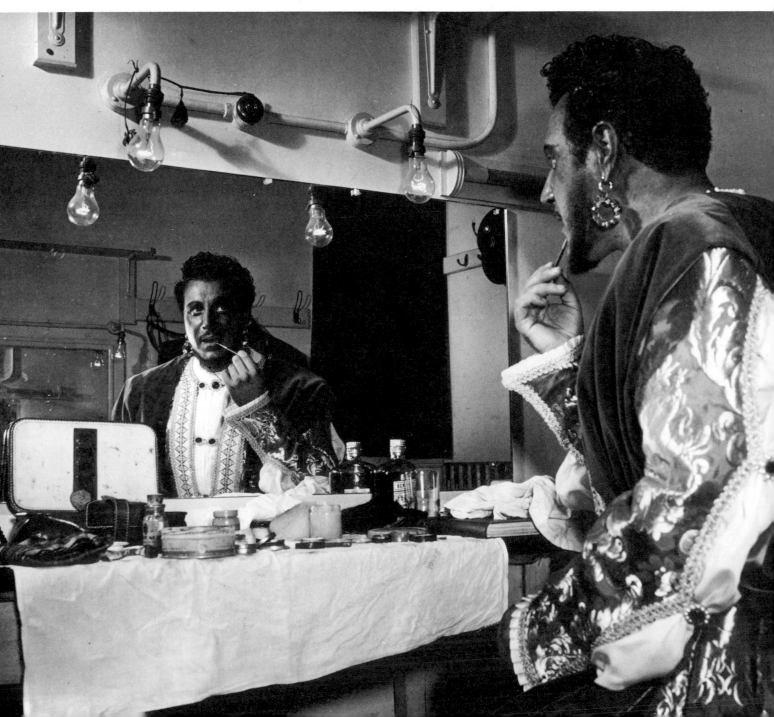

between the two great men must end, because Verdi wrote for the voice and Wagner – some people think – wrote against it, treating it as no more than a different instrument at his command. At all events, Verdi's and the majority of the Italian operatic repertoire is vastly different from the German: more sunny, lighter, and generally possessing pathetic librettos – from the commonsense point of view – and always with good parts for soprano, tenor and baritone or bass. The motivation in Italian opera is far more obvious too, and every opera we know has either an important love element or is based entirely upon it. Except for Humperdinck's *Hansel und Gretel*, Pfitzner's *Palestrina*, Poulenc's *Les Dialogues des Carmelites* and Mussorgsky's *Boris Godunov* in the original version, the Italian style of love flourishes with more abandon.

There is also no shortage of spectacle in Italian opera. Alfredo Catalani's *La Wally* ends with an avalanche, Amilcare Ponchielli's *La Gioconda* calls for a ship to be set on fire, and *Otello* begins with a hurricane on the coast of Cyprus and the arrival of a sailing ship at the port. *Aida* ('the last grand opera') is perhaps the grandest of all. It is made out of processions, crowds of captured soldiers, the betrayal of an army in the desert, hot love and jealousy under the palm trees, and an entombment of Egypt's generalissimo for treason. *Aida* is sometimes performed in Italy outside the opera house, in the arena. Then there is the greatest possibility for pageantry in addition to that already built in. Elephants, camels, hundreds of extras augment the processions, and the spectacle can be made to resemble a tattoo if the producer is not careful to remember that, *au fond*, it is still an opera! Certainly it is a welcome chance to bring it all out from behind the proscenium arch.

Aida was one of Verdi's last three operas, and was followed by *Otello* before his ultimate masterpiece, *Falstaff*. *Otello* is virtually indestructible in performance, and this is a factor which we must sometimes regretfully observe when witnessing badly sung and staged performances, although never actively anticipate them. For that night the magic might work and the glorious old balloon become airborne after all.

There was once a production of *Otello* at La Scala, Milan, which incorporated a glorious moment of perfectly co-ordinated staging and timing. After a short scene in the third act when Otello sees his wife's handkerchief in Cassio's hand and is finally convinced that she is unfaithful to him, offstage trumpets and a ship's cannon announce the arrival on Cyprus of Lodovico, the Venetian ambas-

Madame Butterfly *(Puccini-Giocosa, Illica). Marie Collier in the title role from the 1961 production at Covent Garden*

sador. So from a picture of Iago and Otello in a dark set, planning dark deeds, we seemed instantly to be transported to Lodovico's presence, surrounded by the whole population of the island and in broad sunshine. It was achieved by a complete blackout for no more than four seconds, during which the flimsy back-cloth for the Iago–Otello scene was hoisted away, and all available lights came on as the huge chorus – already in position – started to sing their greeting. Split-second timing was necessary: the orchestra could not stop playing and wait. There was no time for a single mistake. It was stunning. But the worst part of it all must have been (always is!) getting the chorus into position with a minimum of talking and undue movement.

The rightful and immediate heir to Verdi's position in Italian opera was Giacomo Puccini, who had an enormous talent for memorable tunes and stage-worthiness of his operas. But there is a gulf between Verdi and Puccini which the universal decline in awareness of true style and fine cultural perception has done much to mask. There is an innate earthiness, often vulgarity, in Puccini's operas, with the one shining exception of *La Bohème*; vulgarity in music, in the characters and in the situations pertains, so that some people find some of the melodies in *Madame Butterfly* positively insidious, so persuasively do they lodge in the mind and repeat themselves like musical radishes. Of all

The gardens at Glyndebourne with the House and Opera House in the background

Puccini's operas, *Tosca* is perhaps the most repugnantly attractive. In it the producer has great opportunities to create magnificent stage pictures, especially towards the end of the first act which takes place inside the church of Sant' Andrea in Rome. Baron Scarpia, the Chief of Police, enters the church and frightens the life out of some clerics and acolytes who are larking about. But we all know that he is on the track of the hero (the tenor) whom he wishes to implicate in revolutionary activities so that he can snatch his mistress, the actress Tosca, for himself. So his entrance must be spine-chilling.

In the magnificent production at Covent Garden and the Paris Opéra for Maria Callas – her last appearance at both houses – Zeffirelli's sets achieved authenticity and impact – two attributes which do not always coincide. Tito Gobbi was Scarpia, but instead of making his entrance upstage where the audience could see him a fraction in advance of the characters in the opera, he was brought on rather far downstage. His fearful presence had to be imparted to the audience with all the dramatic power at this great singing actor's command. Fortunately he possessed a great deal and it worked, but how much surer the moment would have been had he been able to appear from a more authoritative point.

At the end of *Tosca*, the heroine, who has been tricked and cheated by Scarpia,

sees her lover shot dead before her eyes, and commits suicide by leaping off the top of a tower of the Castel Sant'Angelo. On one occasion the soprano, who was of ample proportions, insisted upon a generously comfortable mattress being placed below the 'tower' for her to land on – perhaps only a few feet below the point from which she jumped. So, flinging herself into space, she duly landed on the mattress, which responded more like a trampoline, propelling her into the air once more, in sight of the audience. It was only on her third contact with the mattress that she was secured by a tactful dresser and persuaded to take no more of these somewhat original calls.

Opera seems to be divided to the extent of about 45 per cent Italian and Italianate, 45 per cent German and Germanic, and 10 per cent for the remainder, world-wide. Among these, there are definite French, English and Russian schools, and of the latter none is more striking than Mussorgsky's *Boris Godunov*. It is a rugged tapestry of Russian history: colourful, cruel and rough-hewn in its original version. It begins outside the Kremlin where a starving crowd has to be brought under control and ends with a snow-clad plain across which revolutionary troops follow their new leader, the pretender Dimitri. An idiot is left symbolically alone in the wastes to mourn the latest turn in his nation's tragic history. In between, we witness the ascent to power, coronation and gradual mental disintegration of the tyrant Tsar Boris, and the coronation scene is – or should be – one of the grandest and most splendid scenes in all Russian opera. The Kremlin's massive bells toll out, the domes and spires of Moscow glow with pure gold, the Tsar's clothing is the last word in opulence and magnificence, well set off by the red coats and tall hats of the twelve members of the Duma, or parliament.

Boris Godunov brings us to Sergei Diaghilev, for it was one of his greatest operatic triumphs, both in Paris and in London, when he introduced the great Chaliapin to Western Europe in the title role. It was Diaghilev who showed Western Europe what a complete production can be. Formerly we were used to getting hold of some scenery, finding some more-or-less suitable costumes, and throwing the singers on to the stage where they sang with little emphasis upon dramatic style or characterisation. So long as they sang prettily, all was well. But there had been no cohesion, no co-ordination, no overall judgement. This is where Diaghilev excelled. For although he was neither poet nor composer, he was extremely musical, played the piano well, had an extremely fine eye for colour and shape, and was an expert on a wide range of works of art. Furthermore, what he brought to Paris was his own company, and it contained the finest singers (and dancers) from Russia, not merely a 'pick-up' team of artists whose different approach would have been sufficiently interesting, but those of the highest calibre, like Chaliapin. Furthermore he commissioned new works himself. If they displeased him, he altered them. And he had a useful instruction to his stage designers which he also applied, metaphorically, to his producers: 'This season, paint it twice as brightly as last.'

No one has ever matched Diaghilev in the ability to be the impresario *par excellence*. Perhaps the nearest has been Rudolph Bing, very successful general manager of Glyndebourne, the Edinburgh Festival and the Metropolitan Opera, New York. The days of impresarios are fast waning, yet there is one man who may lay claim to being the organiser, promoter, composer, conductor and pianist of an annual festival in England. This takes place every summer at the East Anglian fishing town of Aldeburgh, and the man is Benjamin Britten. Although much of the actual administration is no longer his responsibility, for which he must be grateful, he is now the sole impresario-artist remaining in this century. And just occasionally the voice from the darkness may be Britten's.

VI The Great Operas

There are altogether about 4,000 recognised operas of which roughly 100 constitute the regular annual repertoire. Each of those discussed here is superlative in its own right, although many others have vied for a place in this personal selection. The choice includes all the basic ingredients necessary for a work of art, and covers the Italian love of passion, the German aspiration to conquer, the French taste for a coloured narrative, the Russian need for national melodrama, and the Englishman's tradition of restrained emotion.

Three giants among operatic composers are undoubtedly Mozart, Verdi and Wagner. Mozart sees further into the minds of men than any other, and transforms a trivial domestic scene into the universal, even perhaps the sublime. Verdi is the master of human rhythms: love, jealousy, death – and frivolity. Wagner can stir intellectual emotions and astonish by his use of every available resource: orchestra, singers, scenery, machinery, lighting, stage magic, and by his own remarkable fund of knowledge coupled with a grand scale of vision.

Aida

Opera by Giuseppe Verdi in four acts from a plot by Mariette Bey, put into French prose by C. du Locle, thence into the libretto by A. Ghislanzoni. First performed Cairo, 24 December 1871.

Towards the end of his life, Verdi entered into a new and rich phase of composition in which he produced *Aida*, the Requiem Mass, *Otello* (*q.v.*) and *Falstaff* (*q.v.*). *Aida* stands at the beginning of this span of twenty-two years, when Verdi was fifty-eight. 'The last grand opera' embodies such pageant and spectacle that as well as five strong solo voices it can easily accommodate 500 extras. The principals are Amneris, daughter of the King of Egypt, who is in love with Radamès, General of the Egyptian Army against the Ethiopians, who is in love with Aida, captured Ethiopian slave to Amneris, who is really a princess. There are also Amonasro, Aida's father and King of Egypt, and Ramfis the High Priest of Egypt. The opera is about the triangle of love, Amneris, Radamès, Aida, as well as a conflict between Egyptian Church and State. In a moving and dramatic scene Amneris pleads in vain to the High Priest for Radamès' life. He intended to desert to Ethiopia with Aida, thereby delivering his army into enemy hands, but was stopped by Amneris in the nick of time. His punishment is death by suffocation and starvation in an underground tomb. Aida has already found her way there and dies with him while Amneris prays for their peace in the next world.

The opera was commissioned for the opening of the Italian Theatre in Cairo, incidentally in the same year as the opening of the Suez Canal. Mariette Bey's knowledge of Egyptology enabled him to invest the story with true atmosphere, although sometimes the motivation of Radamès is suspect. Verdi, in turn, has captured the sound of whispering palms beside the Nile, the shimmering reflection of the moon on the water and the burning heat of the sand by day. The score is divided into recognisable arias and set-piece numbers including the rousing Triumphal March, Radamès' taxing opening solo 'Celeste Aida', Aida's scena 'Ritorna Vincitor!', and the final love duet. The Nile Scene of Act III holds the greatest cohesion as an act, for it moves fast and has a most exciting curtain after some marvellous music and personal anguish for Aida, Radamès and Amonasro, showing that Verdi was able to bring his characters well forward of the panoply and grandeur of the opera's background and allow them – despite their titles – to register as individuals, as ordinary human beings.

Il Barbiere di Siviglia

Opera by Gioacchino Rossini in two acts to a text by Cesare Sterbini after Beaumarchais' comedy. First performed Teatro Argentina, Rome, 20 February 1816.

Rossini's 'Barber' was at first called *Almaviva, or the Useless Precaution* to differentiate it from Paisiello's opera of 1782 which was still very popular in Italy. The Rossini work was a resounding failure at its first performance owing to a jealous Paisiello claque, but completely successful thereafter. The original overture was lost and the one used now had already been used twice before, while the opera took Rossini no more than thirteen days to compose. It is a vastly superior work to Paisiello's and is probably the funniest of all operas. Rossini's comic invention seems endless, his dry methods of underlining the complications in the plot and events leading to them are particularly endearing. Although this Almaviva and Rosina are very different characters from those we meet later on in Mozart's *Figaro* (*q.v.*) – in any case not strictly an operatic sequel – the character delineation of them and the others on a different plane, without social implications, elevates Rossini's 'Barber' to a masterpiece of the utmost refinement. His 'freezing' of the action when individuals voice their own

Aida at the Metropolitan Opera, New York. Left to right: Bonaldo Giaiotti (High Priest), Marilyn Horne (Amneris), James Morris (the King), James McCracken (Radamès, kneeling), Leontyne Price (Aida)

Above: Il Barbiere di Siviglia *(Rossini–Sterbini). Title page of first edition of the score showing Rosina and Almaviva on either side and Dr Bartolo being shaved by Figaro in the centre at the top*

Right: Il Barbiere di Siviglia. *The Shaving Scene from the 1960 Covent Garden production with Fernando Corena as Dr Bartolo, Teresa Berganza as Rosina hidden behind him, Luigi Alva as Almaviva dressed as the music master and Rolando Panerai as Figaro*

La Bohème *(Puccini–Illica). The 1961 Sadler's Wells production with Elizabeth Vaughan, Wendy Baldwin, William Mcalpine, and Neil Mason*

Far right: Allessandro Bonci as Rodolfo in La Bohème

sentiments in ensemble, his careful vocal balance together with featherweight accompaniment, the gay pulse of the whole work – all these accomplishments continually amaze and delight the listener.

Rossini wrote the role of Rosina for a coloratura mezzo-contralto, though more often it is taken by a soprano. The kind of tenor for Almaviva is also difficult to cast, a graceful, lyric voice with manliness and flexibility. The manipulator of events, Figaro the barber, is less demanding vocally than in needing a strong and winning personality. The *buffo* basses of Dr Bartolo (Rosina's guardian) who loses her to Almaviva after many escapades, and that of Don Basilio, an intriguing music master, both need expert handling if they are not to appear and sound grotesque. In brief, Count Almaviva disguises himself as a drunken soldier, then as a music teacher in order to gain admittance to the house where Rosina is kept in isolation by Dr Bartolo who wants to marry her. By enlisting the invaluable assistance of Figaro, and by bribing Don Basilio, Almaviva achieves his ambition, despite confusion as to his identity in Rosina's mind. A notary arrives and quickly marries Almaviva and Rosina with Basilio as witness, right under Bartolo's nose. It is full of excellent clowning, funny voices and the speed of a French farce.

La Bohème
Opera by Giacomo Puccini in four acts after Henri Murger's novel *Scènes de la Vie de Bohème* to a libretto by Giacosa and L. Illica. First performed Teatro Regio, Turin, 1 February 1896 (conducted by Toscanini).

La Bohème is Puccini's fourth opera but the first to show his complete maturity of style. Its first performance was a failure but from its third production in 1896 it has been indisputably successful. When Puccini heard that Leoncavallo was at work on the same subject, he brought his version out first in time to get it fully established. Leoncavallo's *La Bohème* has been completely eclipsed.

Puccini sets the scene most adroitly, and although he was no Parisian, he creates an authentic idiom. Four Bohemians live in a cold attic, Marcello (a painter), Rodolfo (a poet), Schaunard (a musician) and Colline (a philosopher). After some horseplay and the burning of Rodolfo's verses instead of a chair in an effort to keep warm, all but Rodolfo go out to the local Café Momus. A neighbour, Mimi, asks him for a light for she has lost her key. As they look for it their hands touch, and this leads to a declaration of love. In the second act, Mimi and Rodolfo have joined his friends at the café, when Musetta, once Marcello's mistress, arrives with a wealthy old man called Alcindoro – much to Marcello's discomfort. But when he and Musetta make it up and go away together, so do all the other Bohemians, leaving Alcindoro with their bill. At the 'Barrière des Enfers' in Act III, we are made aware of Mimi's failing health, while the aimless life of the Bohemians is made clearer than ever. The last act begins in the same way as Act I, when Musetta suddenly arrives with Mimi, who is dying. Colline sells his precious overcoat to buy medicine for her, but too late. Rodolfo is looking out of the window while the others stand round Mimi's corpse. It is only when he turns round and sees their faces that he too realises that she is dead.

Apart from Puccini's farcical opera, *Gianni Schicchi*, *La Bohème* is the only one in which he avoids sheer cruelty in the plot. It is generous and warmhearted; a tragedy, of course, but among little people whom we easily recognise. In their enforced gaiety and carefree habits this tragedy is magnified. The dialogue is beautifully handled in the music, melodious and natural, while the big musical moments that follow each other rapidly have earned the opera its fame and success. They are the extended duet between Mimi and Rodolfo at the end of Act I; Musetta's Waltz Song in Act II; Mimi's aria 'Donde lieta usci' in Act III, followed by the Quartet; Colline's song to his coat; and the tragic finale.

Boris Godunov

Opera by Modeste Mussorgsky in a prologue and four acts. Text by the composer after Alexander Pushkin's drama. First complete performance St Petersburg, 8 February 1874.

This is one of Russia's great national operas – about the People. It was Mussorgsky's only completed opera score among seven unfinished ones, but even so it was in several forms, following revisions and second thoughts of Mussorgsky. Furthermore, after his death, Rimsky-Korsakov re-orchestrated and remoulded it, smoothing out the primitive harmonies and orchestral effects and thereby changing its immediate flavour. So any of several productions with a number of different scenes can still be performed and called authentic. It is a page of violent Russian history, starting with the protestations of Boris Godunov when asked to become Tsar. He has murdered Prince Dmitri, who stood in his way to the throne, but has pangs of conscience. Finally a crowd outside the Kremlin persuade him to accept and his magnificent coronation scene follows. Meanwhile, in a monastery far away, an old monk, Pimen, is writing a history of Russia. A novice learns much about recent events from him and decides to assume the personality of the murdered Dmitri and challenge Boris's right to the throne. Accompanied by two drunken friars, Varlaam and Missail, he manages to trick his way across the Lithuanian border into Russia. One of the Boyars, Shuisky, informs Boris of this and 'sets his mind at rest' by recounting the manner of Dmitri's death. This has the opposite effect upon Boris who suffers a hallucinatory vision. Sometimes, for the sake of a romantic soprano part and a love scene (which otherwise do not exist) a Polish Scene is inserted here when the false Dmitri secures the support of Marina, a Polish Princess, on promise of marriage. Their duet at a fountain is far more Rimsky than Mussorgsky. Also, in this case, there is a scheming monk, Rangoni, Princess Marina's confessor, who hopes to advance the Catholic cause in Russia. The opera's last two scenes may be performed with either first: the Council Scene, at which Boris has a stroke and dies, or the Revolution Scene, when the false Dmitri leads his rabble army towards Moscow and an Idiot bewails the sad lot of the Russian people. Since it is an opera about the people, this scene, with the Idiot's wailing, high tenor voice, makes a more fitting conclusion.

Célestine Galli-Marié, the creator of Carmen in 1875 at the Paris Opéra Comique

Opposite: Boris Christoff as Boris Godunov, a role in which the Bulgarian bass has excelled since he first sang it at Covent Garden in 1949

Carmen

Opéra-comique by Georges Bizet in four acts after Prosper Merimée's novel. Text by Henri Meilhac and Ludovic Halévy. First performed Paris, Opéra-Comique, 3 March 1875.

This was Bizet's last opera, an outstanding example of opéra-comique (with its spoken dialogue), and of the *verismo* style which was soon to become established in Italy. It was the first opera to show cigarette-smoking upon the stage, and in spite of its cast of common soldiers, factory girls, gypsies, bandits, and crowds at a bull-fight, it avoids being tawdry. The only character of any stature is Escamillo, the reigning toreador, but he is two-dimensional by comparison with Carmen and Don José, the two main characters in the story. Prosper Merimée's tale comes through the libretto with far more impact than in the episodic novel, while Bizet's use of authentic rhythms and dances seem really Spanish and not merely Spain *à la française*. It is earthy, savage, filled with hot passion and blood. The most evocative performance which the author ever witnessed was at Le Carré, Amsterdam, immediately following a circus performance whose smell lingered. Yet even without the titillation of an extra sense, *Carmen*'s music is elevated, virile and so powerful that other versions of 'Carmen' in ballet, musical comedy and film pay great tribute to the original work and leave it unscathed by imitation. The four acts are each well contrasted

Carmen *(Bizet–Meilhac, Halévy).*
The scene in Act I when street
urchins mock the soldiers as they
drill

Don Giovanni *(Mozart-Da Ponte).*
Peter Glossop in the title role.
Covent Garden 1973

in mood and in time of day or night, light and darkness, emphasising the tragedy which is expressed most poignantly by very ordinary people. The core of the story is about the love of a selfish gypsy girl for a corporal, and his unnecessary destruction when she loves someone else. The fact that he kills her out of jealousy is less important than his total degradation.

Dido and Aeneas

Opera by Henry Purcell in a prologue and three acts to a text by Nahum Tate from Virgil's *Aeneid*, Book IV. First performance in the garden of Josias Priest's School for Young Gentlewomen, Leicester Fields, London, either late 1689 or summer 1690.

Purcell's unique opera is considered to be a work of genius, making it all the more regrettable that his other works for the theatre were restricted to incidental music and masques. *Dido and Aeneas* is the first true English opera, of such skill, integrity and maturity that any operas being written in Europe at the same time seem puny beside it. After *Dido*'s few, rare productions up to the beginning of the eighteenth century, it was not seen for 100 years. Purcell's style, insight, beauty of orchestral texture and meaning which completely fused the text to his score, were all overlooked in favour of the two-dimensional fashions, by comparison so shallow. Several versions of Purcell's opera exist because of the licence to alter, transpose or otherwise interfere with works of art; and because the earliest texts differ from one another, it is impossible to discover exactly which form the first performance took, or upon what date it was given.

The story tells how Aeneas has escaped from Troy after its capture, and is on his way to Italy, as ordered by the gods, when he puts in at Carthage. There Queen Dido falls in love with him and at the beginning of Purcell's opera she is seen soliloquising upon her inability to declare her feelings to him. Her confi-

dante, Belinda, and her Carthaginian courtiers persuade her in Aeneas' presence to unite their kingdoms. They all praise Love and Beauty. A Sorceress and Chorus of Witches plan the downfall of Carthage and of Dido (whom they refer to as 'Elissa'). They raise a storm and separate the lovers while they are out hunting, and an Elf, disguised as the God Mercury, impresses Aeneas with his obligation to leave for Italy as if it were again Jove's command. At the harbour Aeneas's sailors are glad to be leaving Carthage, and the Witches are delighted at their success, intending to sink Aeneas's fleet and set the city on fire. Dido appears, grief-stricken, and scornfully dismisses the still vacillating Aeneas. Her great lament 'When I am laid in earth' is her farewell to him and to life. The final scene shows a Chorus of Cupids guarding her tomb eternally.

Dido and Aeneas (Purcell-Tate). Kirsten Flagstad as Dido in the 1950 production at the Mermaid Theatre, St John's Wood

Don Giovanni

Dramma giocosa by Wolfgang Amadeus Mozart, sometimes called an *opera buffa*, in two acts after the legend by a Spanish monk, Tirso de Molinar, to a libretto by Lorenzo da Ponte. First performed Prague, National Theatre, 29 October 1787.

Don Giovanni is a compulsive seducer of women. The overture to this grandly romantic opera sets an ominous scene proclaiming its prophecy of doom. The trombone blasts signify the Don's boldness and the parallel whole-tone scales tell of avenging retribution, calculated to fill the audience with apprehension before the curtain has gone up. When it does so it is to a flippant note with Leporello, the Don's manservant, complaining about overtime. Then suddenly Donna Anna rushes in. The Don has raped her. The distinguished Commendatore, her father, runs on sword in hand to engage the Don and is struck down. The music of the ensuing trio between the dying Commendatore, the Don and Leporello most poignantly expresses the old man's pathetic end and points to further tragedy. Don Giovanni's past amorous exploits are shown by the be-

117

Right: Elektra (Strauss-
Hofmannsthal). London première
of a new Strauss opera on 19
February 1910 conducted by Mr
Thomas Beecham and with
Friedrich Weidemann as Orest,
Edyth Walker as Elektra and
Anna Bahr-Mildenburg as
Clytemnestra

Below: Elektra *world première at
Dresden on 25 January 1900,
showing Ernestine Schumann-
Heink as Clytemnestra and Anny
Krull as Elektra*

trayed Donna Elvira, who is pursuing him relentlessly for revenge; by Leporello's account of his master's escapades; and by his compulsive pursuit of the next woman he sees, a country girl called Zerlina. The Don temporarily outwits her swain, Masetto, but at a party he gives at his own house is prevented by the masked Anna, Don Ottavio (her fiancé) and Elvira, now agents of human retribution, from having his way with Zerlina. He is cornered, but escapes. He pursues his course to a cemetery where the Commendatore's statue accepts his flippant invitation to supper. He laughs it off, yet prepares for his stone guest who does in fact arrive. Fearlessly Giovanni accepts the statue's icy handshake, and, still refusing to repent, he is dragged down to Hell.

Mozart's invention combined with Da Ponte's ingenious libretto have given opportunities for endless controversy about the plot: whether the Don is only a reckless womaniser, whether he feels anything deeper, whether he is merely bored or is driven by some demon in his collecting hobby. Each character remains identifiable yet they are all blended by Mozart to express every emotion from sublimity to horror. *Don Giovanni* is unsurpassed as an opera for its range of passions.

Elektra

Opera by Richard Strauss in one act to a libretto by Hugo von Hofmannsthal after his own play-adaptation of Sophocles' drama. First performed Dresden, Royal Opera House, 25 January 1909.

At the outset the orchestra blares out: 'Agamemnon!' – the name of the murdered King of Argos whose unquiet spirit broods over the city, waiting for his death to be avenged. His widow Clytemnestra, who slew him with the aid of her effeminate lover, Aegisthus, now rules Argos despotically with Aegisthus. Electra, Clytemnestra's elder daughter, is treated like an animal and is kept alive only by her burning passion: to wait for her brother Orestes' return to avenge their father. Electra's sister, Chrysothemis (not Iphigenie in this version of the story) longs for marriage and children. She sympathises with Electra but will not help her. Clytemnestra is mentally and physically ill, and has fearful nightmares. Electra taunts her by announcing her mother's impending death. When a messenger brings news that Orestes is dead, Clytemnestra is relieved, Electra is thus resolved to slay her mother and step-father herself. While she is looking for the very axe which killed Agamemnon, a human shadow falls across her. It is a stranger who assures her that Orestes is not dead at all, and after some conversation he is revealed as Orestes, though Electra will not allow him to embrace her. He must go and do the deed for which he has come. Orestes is less resolved than his sister but cannot hesitate in the face of her fanaticism, and enters the palace. After a moment of extreme tension, Clytemnestra's death cries are heard. When Aegisthus enters, Electra is, for once, charmingly polite to him and lights his way. He cannot understand her change of attitude, and goes inside – to his death. The palace is in an uproar but those who support Orestes and Electra are victorious. She is crazed by the events, and now without any purpose in life, does a dance of triumph and collapses, dead. Chrysothemis beats at the closed palace doors, calling for Orestes.

In this opera Strauss advanced the recognised form of tonality so far that, like Orestes, he was standing upon the very edge of familiar surroundings, ready to assault the whole fabric of law and order. It is idle to conjecture what might have arisen had he gone further. Instead he retraced his steps to the comfortable surroundings of Vienna in *Der Rosenkavalier* (*q.v.*). *Elektra* was the first in the Strauss–Hofmannsthal partnership of six operas in just over twenty years, and is the most economical in what it achieves through imaginative strokes by both its creators. It is a one-act masterpiece without rival in opera:

Fidelio *(Beethoven–Treitschke), showing Lotte Lehmann as Leonore (right), Franz Völker as Florestan released from prison, and Herbert Janssen as Don Fernando, his deliverer. Covent Garden 1934*

not Greek, not Sophoclean, but still an everlasting story embodying high tensions and with music that clearly and unmistakably underlines the psychological state of each character.

Falstaff

Opera in three acts by Giuseppe Verdi to a text by Arrigo Boito after Shakespeare's play *The Merry Wives of Windsor*. First performed La Scala, Milan, 9 February 1893.

Falstaff adds the last superlative touch to Verdi's operatic output, finished and performed when he was almost eighty years of age. It is full of good humour and complete enjoyment of life, yet exhibits such understanding of the ways of men and women as could have come only after a lifetime's study of them. The libretto is expertly wrought by Boito, follows Shakespeare's play closely and borrows several sentiments and moments from *Henry IV*. The opera falls neatly into six separate scenes, two to each act, with every scene a through-composed dramatic and musical entity. There are a few distinctly recognisable themes: the Anne–Fenton love music; the 'dalle due alle tre' and 'Reverenza!' statements of Mistress Quickly; and the bubbling, yet spiky music of the Merry Wives themselves. This caused criticism of Verdi by anti-Wagnerians who saw a move by the Italian master towards the methods employed at Bayreuth, but it now seems a far-fetched argument, especially as *Falstaff* ends with a fugue, sung by the whole company, not with an aria. If there is any intention of parody, it must surely be at Verdi himself, with this comic take-off of a jealousy subject after his previous opera, *Otello* (q.v.).

In *Falstaff*, the jealous character is Master Ford, a gentleman of Windsor who wants his daughter Anne to marry Dr Caius (an odious person), and most certainly not young Fenton with whom she is in love. Sir John Falstaff, a braggart and tippler, has sent identical letters to two Windsor ladies, Mistress Page and Mistress Ford, proposing assignations. Mistress Quickly brings the answers to Falstaff personally: Alice Ford awaits him that very afternoon between two and three when Ford will be out. Falstaff is highly delighted and when a Master 'Brook' is announced (Ford in disguise and frantic with jealousy, for he has been tipped off about Falstaff's plans) Falstaff falls into the trap and tells Ford that he is off to seduce his wife. The Merry Wives prepare for Falstaff's arrival at Ford's house, but when he arrives his advances are cut short by Ford's return, supported by servants ready to cudgel the fat knight. The women hide him in a laundry basket which is then thrown out of a window into the river Thames. The same evening Falstaff is seen sitting outside his favourite inn trying to cure a cold and lamenting the world's wickedness. Quickly arrives with a second letter from Alice Ford, inviting him to meet her in Windsor Forest at midnight, dressed as Herne the Hunter with horns upon his head. Falstaff rises to the bait and is met by the entire company, some dressed as fairies and all masked, who first tease and then beat him. Through a trick, Ford is persuaded to accept Fenton as his son-in-law, and the opera ends with a monumental orchestral and vocal fugue: 'All the world's a stage'. Falstaff is again the loser, but his vanity and irrepressible nature remain unscathed.

Fidelio

Opera in three acts by Ludwig van Beethoven, after Jean-Nicolas Bouilly's *Léonore, ou l'Amour Conjugal* (based on a true event) to a libretto by Joseph Sonnleithner (1805); reduced to two acts by Stefan von Breuning (1806); put into its final form by Georg Friedrich Treitschke, and staged in this version at the Kärntnertor Theater, Vienna, 23 May 1814.

Beethoven's only opera used a libretto which had already been set by at least three other composers before he wrestled unhappily with it, eventually being persuaded to recast the whole work and to drop several numbers, much against his inclination. The first version was given only three times, while the French army was battering its way towards Vienna in 1805; the final (and usual) version appeared nine years later after Beethoven, realising the worth of what he had done, and the need for revision, said: 'It has decided me once more to rebuild the desolate ruins of an ancient fortress.'

Fidelio is classical in design, a rescue opera in which the *deus ex machina* is an ordinary man. In circumstances of political unrest the heroine, Leonore, dressed as a boy, is searching prisons throughout Spain for her husband Don Florestan. He has been wrongly held captive for over two years by a personal enemy, Don Pizarro, and it is by no means certain to Leonore that he is still alive. When the opera opens in the living-room of the head jailer Rocco's house, Leonore (called Fidelio) is seen as a new apprentice engaged in yet another prison. But Rocco's daughter Marcelline has fallen in love with the 'boy'. Leonore succeeds in persuading Rocco to let her accompany him to the deepest dungeon to dig a grave for a special prisoner, and then she recognises her husband, almost dead from hunger and neglect. When Don Pizarro arrives to kill Florestan, Leonore intervenes and saves him. The Governor arrives in the nick of time, Pizarro is arrested, Florestan and all the other prisoners are released. The last scene of the opera is played in full lighting, after almost continuous preceding gloom, and the symbolic release of Florestan's chains by Leonore herself is done in a static, oratorio-like finale of joy and freedom. (The word *Freiheit* occurs frequently in the opera.)

Victor Maurel, the French baritone, who created the roles Iago in Otello (1887) and Falstaff (1893) both at La Scala, and both at Verdi's special request. He had already created Amonasro in the American première of Aida at the Academy of Music, New York, in 1873. He opened a singing studio in London at the beginning of the century and moved to New York where he taught from 1909 until his death there in 1923

Fidelio exemplifies freedom and the personal dignity of the individual, so that its story and its message are timeless. But it is Beethoven's music which elevates the story to a masterpiece, with its alternating moments of power, tenderness and sublimity; with a complete understanding of the individual characters' *feelings* (as in the Canon Quartet in the first scene) that the music expresses to perfection, yet without the need for *Leitmotive*. Among the most glorious moments, when action and music are fused to achieve perfect descriptive powers, are the Quartet already mentioned, Don Pizarro's outburst of anger and determination, Leonore's scena of disgust (having heard him) giving way to hope, and the prisoners' chorus when they are allowed to see daylight for a moment.

Fidelio has four associated overtures: Leonora No. 1, which was discarded; Leonora Nos 3 and 2, which were used for the premières of the earlier versions in that order, and finally the overture to *Fidelio* which is in a different key so as to lead into the revised opening scene. Sometimes Leonora No. 3 is played as an interlude between the two scenes of Act II, but the musical and dramatic wisdom of doing so is questionable.

Götterdämmerung

Music drama by Richard Wagner in three acts. First performance Festspielhaus, Bayreuth, 17 August 1876.

Götterdämmerung is the fourth and last opera of the monumental cycle *Der Ring des Nibelungen*, for which Wagner wrote libretto and score. The first two operas, *Das Rheingold* and *Die Walküre*, had previously been staged in Munich in 1869 and 1870 respectively, but it was not until Wagner's specially designed theatre was ready that *Siegfried* and *Götterdämmerung* were first heard. The complete cycle was then presented at Bayreuth, under ideal conditions, during 13–17 August 1876. The tetralogy is based on a wide variety of mythological stories and tells of the greedy struggle for power between three races, the gods, dwarfs and giants. The world-hero, Siegfried, whose parents were brother and sister, is brought into the conflict as a pawn of the principal god Wotan. Siegfried has, by Wotan's rules, to act voluntarily, and since he knows no fear until he encounters a woman (Brünnhilde, one of Wotan's daughters reduced to human status for disobedience) he is invincible and wayward. The evil Alberich, chief of the dwarfs and Wotan's foremost adversary, appoints his own son Hagen to trick and slay Siegfried in order to recover from him the golden Ring, token and symbol of world power. But even Alberich cannot prevent its being thrown back into the river Rhine whence he stole it at the start of the first evening of the huge operatic story.

In *Götterdämmerung* we see the enraptured Siegfried and Brünnhilde on the morning after their first meeting, when Siegfried has released her from twenty years of sleep by falling in love with her. He departs on a heroic journey, leaving the Ring with Brünnhilde as token of his faith. He encounters Hagen, evil son of Alberich (and Siegfried's opposite number in the story) who drugs him and destroys his memory. Brünnhilde is seized by a man in Siegfried's shape, who tears the Ring from her finger; she then sees the real Siegfried who swears that he does not know her; and as a result she demonstrates her truly gained womanhood (no longer godhead) by a fit of jealousy. She discloses the only place on Siegfried's body – his back – where he can be killed. Siegfried is killed by Hagen. Wotan's hope of a self-willed hero who will return the Ring to the Rhine has now gone. Brünnhilde is told that Siegfried was true to her, and she rides her horse into the flames of his funeral pyre. These flames consume the gods in Valhalla before the river Rhine rises and quenches them, showing the Rhinemaidens, guardians of the Ring, once again possessing it.

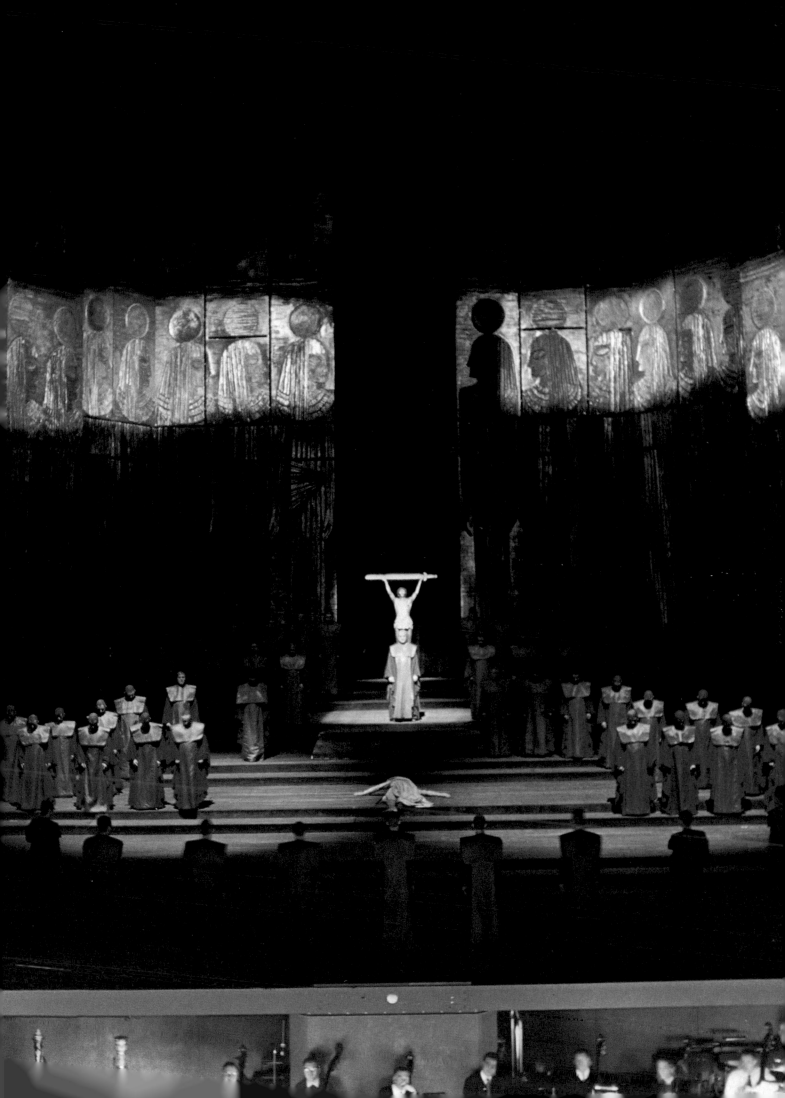

The immensity of the story is compelling in itself, the characters are firmly and clearly drawn, and the story is easy to follow since there is a recapitulation of what has passed in each opera after the first. Wagner makes great use of the *Leitmotive*, a musical label whose meaning remains constant, and the score abounds in richness, in melody and in continuous inventiveness. There has never been another composition like *Der Ring*, of which *Götterdämmerung* is the culmination. It is all conceived on such gigantic lines and achieved so perfectly, that controversy over interpretation of details in its carefully wrought structure, both literary and musical, continues a century later.

Opening scene from Berlioz's Les Troyens à Carthage *with Janet Baker (seated) as Dido, in the 1969 revival at Covent Garden*

L'Incoronazione di Poppea

Opera by Claudio Monteverdi in a prologue and three acts to the libretto by F. Busenello after Tacitus. First performance Venice, Teatro Sancti Giovanni e Paolo, 1642.

The Coronation of Poppea is Monteverdi's crowning glory at the age of seventy-five, and it has been described by a Monteverdian scholar as 'the supreme music drama of the epoch'. It achieved such a complete fusion of the arts that it far outpaced other composers' efforts until the emergence of Gluck, nearly 150 years later. Three aspects of the opera are specially notable: the plot, which in Christian or any moral terms is thoroughly immoral; the use of sub-plots which contribute to the main plot yet do not cloud the action; and the amazing skill with which the monologues and recitatives are dovetailed together to underline the dramatic situations.

The Prologue (sometimes omitted) shows Fortune, Virtue and Amor (Love) arguing as to which is the most powerful. Amor wins. In the first act, Nero, the Roman Emperor (cast originally as a castrato, thus underlining his mental fragility) is married to Ottavia, but is desperately in love with Poppea. She is the wife of Ottone whom Nero has sent abroad on state business so as to get him out of the way. Ottone unexpectedly returns, and finds two of Nero's soldiers asleep outside his house. His cry of anguish at this discovery wakens them, and they confirm his suspicions. Ottone watches Nero take fond leave of Poppea at dawn. Then Arnalta, Poppea's nurse, warns her to beware of Ottavia's jealousy. In a 'mirror scene' Ottavia exhibits intense jealousy and the need for revenge in a duologue with her nurse. She consults the philosopher, Seneca, who upsets her further by advising dignity and virtue. Pallas Athene warns Seneca that he will die that day, and Nero then informs him that he proposes to marry Poppea, having first done away with his wife. Seneca argues sensibly with Nero until the Emperor becomes incensed with rage. Nero's love scene with Poppea is witnessed by Ottone, still in hiding, during which Poppea persuades Nero to have Seneca killed. In another mirror scene, Arnalta, in hiding, watches Ottavia's and Ottone's postponed meeting. The second act starts with Nero's joy at Seneca's death. Ottavia assumes the dignity of Empress and orders Ottone to kill Poppea. He dresses as a woman so as to gain admittance to her room, using the clothes of Drusilla, a young lady who loves him. Amor stands guard over Poppea and repulses Ottone. The alarm is raised, and Drusilla, whose clothes were recognised, is arrested. She is tortured and confesses to the attempted murder of Poppea. Ottone comes forward and also confesses, so impressing Nero that he spares their lives though condemning them both to exile. Poppea realises that the way to her marriage to Nero is now clear and agrees to accept his proposal. Ottavia sings a poignant farewell to Rome and also departs. The Coronation Scene has a chorus of male voices and was Busenello's finale, but Monteverdi added the final, conversational duet between the two lovers, marking so beautifully in music the characters of surely the most odious hero and heroine in all opera.

L'Incoronazione di Poppea
(Monteverdi–Busenello). The
Glyndebourne production of
1962-3-4 showing Richard Lewis
as Nero and Magda Laszlo as
Poppea at their wedding in the
finale of the opera

Die Meistersinger von Nürnberg

Opera by Richard Wagner in three acts to a text by the composer. First performed
Munich, 21 June 1868.

During the twenty years it took him to write and compose *Der Ring*, Wagner
turned his attention to two independent operas, *Tristan und Isolde* (q.v.) and
Die Meistersinger. This is the warmest, most human (in general terms) and most
easily approachable of all Wagner's works.

It is set in sixteenth-century Nuremberg where a young knight, Walther von
Stolzing (a visitor to the city), sees Eva, daughter of Pogner the goldsmith, in
church, and falls in love with her. When he learns that she will be married on
the following day to whoever wins a singing competition, he decides to take
part himself. He is told about the strict rules and performs his extempore song
before the Masters, of whom Pogner is the chairman. Among them is the small-
minded town clerk, Sextus Beckmesser, who is the 'marker' for Walther, and
enjoys noting all the faults on a slate until it is full up. Although the young
knight has failed in his first round and the meeting breaks up, one of the masters,
Hans Sachs the cobbler, shows appreciation of Walther's efforts. That night,
Midsummer's Eve, Sachs is sitting outside his shop working when Eva comes
to him to ask how Walther got on at the trial. Sachs, who loves her too in spite

of being much older, upsets her by teasing and she breaks down. Sachs decides to help the young couple who plan to elope that night, by preventing it – quite the wrong thing to do – and lights up the street in front of his shop. Beckmesser comes to serenade Eva, as he is already sure of his success, and Sachs keeps up an accompaniment of hammering on a shoe, 'marking' Beckmesser as he had earlier marked Walther. The noise wakes up the townsfolk who beat up Beckmesser and once more prevent Eva and Walther from leaving. Sachs is soliloquising the next morning about the world's madness, as well as about Eva and Walther's love, when the knight arrives to tell the cobbler of a song he had dreamed. It is the prize song, though without the final stanza. Sachs writes it down and leaves his manuscript on the table while he goes to change for the contest. Beckmesser limps in, still bruised from the night before, and steals the song. Eva calls to have a shoe mended, but really to see Walther, and their meeting inspires him to finish the song. In the great quintet they 'christen' David, Sachs's newly appointed journeyman, who loves Eva's nurse, Magdalena, the fifth voice. The final scene on the banks of the river Pegnitz is one of gaiety and ceremony, showing the arrival of many different guilds and apprentices. Sachs presides and the first contestant is Beckmesser, who makes a complete hash of Walther's song. When he angrily accuses Sachs of having written it, the cobbler introduces its real composer, Walther von Stolzing, to demon-

strate how it should really be sung. Walther wins the prize, but at first rejects the golden chain of the guild. But Sachs reminds him of the guild's purpose: to preserve and honour the art of German song. Eva takes the victor's wreath from Walther's head and places it upon Sachs's amidst great jubilation.

Die Meistersinger is something of a German national opera and is an utterly peaceful work in which the character of Hans Sachs comes through as benign, self-sacrificing and generous. Beckmesser is Wagner's only comic character, and his singing of nonsense words to an appalling tune in the contest can be very funny indeed. The opera is well constructed and balanced and, apart from the Prize Song and the Quintet, Sachs's two monologues, at the beginning of Act II and of Act III, are masterpieces of reflective musical expression.

Götterdämmerung *(Wagner). The killing of Siegfried by Hagen. An evocative, swirling lighting effect, depicting disaster and chaos*

127

*Die Meistersinger von Nürnberg
(Wagner). Jess Thomas as
Walther von Stolzing faces the
Masters for his first trial in Act I.
Covent Garden 1969*

Sketch for Act II of the original production of Die Meistersinger, *Munich 1868*

Set design for Norma *Act I (the Sacred Grove) by Pier Luigi Pizzi*

Norma

Opera by Vincenzo Bellini in two acts to a text by Felice Romani after Louis Alexandre Soumet's tragedy. First performance La Scala, Milan, 26 December 1831.

Norma is a classical tragedy in a romantic setting, which embodies nobility of character with true pathos. All this is matched and heightened in Bellini's score, which follows in the musical line of the German composers. This may explain why Wagner was so taken with it, recognising a complete union of words and music, and inspiring him to compose a 'Libertà' aria in the style of Bellini for a production of the opera, set for tenor and chorus.

The action takes place in Gaul where the Druids, ruled by their High Priest Oroveso and his priestess daughter Norma, wish to rise up against the Roman invaders. Pollione, the proconsul, has fathered two children by Norma – ostensibly a virgin – but he now turns his affection towards Adalgisa, another Druid priestess. In a passionate scene, Pollione tries to persuade Adalgisa to go to Rome with him. Norma senses Pollione's coldness towards her but does not yet realise who her rival is. Adalgisa confesses to Norma that she has betrayed her priestess's vows by loving a Roman, and is about to be released from them by the sympathetic Norma when Pollione joins them and everything at once becomes clear to them all. Adalgisa rejects Pollione by remaining true to Norma, who in desperation plans to kill her children. But she cannot do it and gives them instead to Adalgisa's care, hoping that Pollione will return to her. When a message from him declares that he will not, Norma in cold rage summons the Druids and agrees to make war on the Romans. This scene of the woman scorned, striking a huge bronze gong as a sign of battle, is of truly heroic proportions. Pollione is captured by the Druids and is offered his freedom by Norma in return for his love. He refuses and she reveals her guilt to the

130

appalled assembly. Her punishment is death by fire, and when her distraught and broken father, Oroveso, takes charge of the funeral pyre, Pollione is so impressed by her strength of character that he accompanies her through the flames and dies with her.

The most perfect musical number in the opera is Norma's scena 'Casta Diva' where she restrains her subjects' anger and prays for peace with Rome. The great trio which expresses recrimination from Norma and Adalgisa towards Pollione, and his self-justification, is elegantly and faithfully caught by Bellini, as is the duet in thirds between Norma and Adalgisa in the second act, once rejected (strangely enough) by public opinion. The finale is the crown to the whole, expressing Oroveso's grief, Norma's integrity, the Druids' horror and admiration, and Pollione's last act which almost redeems him as a person.

Le Nozze di Figaro

Opera by Wolfgang Amadeus Mozart in four acts to text by Lorenzo da Ponte after Beaumarchais' comedy of the same name. First performance Vienna, Burgtheater, 1 May 1786.

Pierre Augustin Caron de Beaumarchais wrote his *Barber of Seville* (*q.v.*) before the French Revolution, and *The Marriage of Figaro after* it. While *Figaro* stands, to a certain extent, as a sequel to the earlier piece, its characters are all a good deal older, and it is the social framework to their lives that has changed the most. If the play of *Figaro* is to be regarded as frivolous, Mozart's opera is certainly not. It is *sui generis*: the first 'conversational' opera.

It opens with Figaro measuring a room and Susanna, the Countess's maid, trying on a hat while they discuss their wedding preparations. The Countess Rosina has become a serious and tragic figure, rejected by the amorous, middle-aged Count Almaviva, while the new and entrancing character of Cherubino, a young page to the Count, is the first breeches-role in opera. Mozart has heightened and ennobled the passions of these people by the music he has given them; and while the opera has a comic tinge, it is high comedy without any trace of vulgarity. Furthermore, the people in it tend to learn from one another's mistakes in the course of the action, and to become changed by its end, so making the opera a profound social comment. The opera was such a success when first produced in Vienna, and then in Prague, that the composer was invited to Prague where, in his own words, 'the one topic of conversation here is – *Figaro*; nothing is played sung or whistled but – *Figaro*; no one goes to any other opera but – *Figaro*; everlasting *Figaro*!'

The story tells how the marriage between Figaro and Susanna is beset with difficulties. The Count has decided to make her the subject of his next conquest while Figaro is obliged to marry Marcellina if he cannot discharge a debt of money to her. The amorous page Cherubino is found by the Count in a compromising situation, but the Count is caught off guard while chasing Susanna. So Cherubino is punished by being sent to join the army. In a scene of great fun and excitement, Cherubino has to hide again to avoid the Count, but by jumping from a window and breaking some plants is in further danger until Figaro takes the blame. Susanna pretends to yield to the Count when he tells her that he will force Figaro to marry Marcellina, but when it is discovered that she and Bartolo are Figaro's parents, no one can prevent Susanna's marriage to Figaro except the Count. Susanna and the Countess change clothes in order to shame the Count and to stop his pursuit of Susanna once and for all. When the Count finds that he is making love to his own wife and Figaro discovers that he is addressing the Countess there is general confusion. The Count is reluctantly obliged to ask everybody's pardon and the opera ends happily in this new world of social 'equality'.

Kathleen Ferrier as Orpheus in the Covent Garden production especially mounted for her in 1953, with Sir John Barbirolli conducting. She collapsed after the second performance on 6 February and died eight months later

Orfeo ed Euridice

Azione teatrale per musica by Christoph Willibald Gluck in three acts to a text by Raniero di Calzabigi after the classical Greek legend. First (Vienna) version, Burgtheater, 5 October 1762. Second (Paris) version, Académie, 2 August 1774.

In 1760 Gluck was working in Vienna with the poet Metastasio as his librettist. Two years later he felt strong enough to break from the outworn operatic conventions, and, taking Calzabigi as his librettist, worked closely with him on *Orfeo ed Euridice*. Their collaboration was responsible for a number of innovations: arias which grew out of the action with sufficient strength to be shorn of all artificial embellishment; a chorus that played a positive part in the drama; and a terse version of the story with only two principals and the Spirit of Love. This economy of forces underlined Gluck's own spare musical resources as well as the need to adapt them more truthfully to the story. Although all this was probably not appreciated at the time, it nevertheless led to acceptance of Gluck's operatic reforms. The two versions are often merged in performance today except for one difference. Orfeo was sung in Vienna by the castrato Guadagni; in Paris (where no castrati were allowed) by the tenor Legros. Indeed, in Paris Gluck's detractors claimed that Guardagni had composed *Orfeo*. The Paris version included some remarkable additions: the flute solo and dance of the Blessèd Spirits, the dance of the Furies and the Air for Euridice with Chorus. Today the role of Orfeo is taken by a contralto, although on rare occasions when a baritone is cast, the effect is quite different from that which Gluck intended. The story is the familiar one of the great love between Orfeo and his wife Euridice who dies and goes down to Hades. Because Orfeo is beloved of the gods for his musical ability he is allowed to retrieve her on condition that he never looks at her again. He successfully passes all dangers by playing his lyre and calming the evil spirits. But at the mouth of Hades he unthinkingly looks round to make sure that his wife is following, only to behold her being dragged back there for ever.

Otello

Opera by Giuseppe Verdi in three acts based on Shakespeare's play to a libretto by Arrigo Boito. First performance La Scala, Milan, 5 February 1887.

Otello is the best example of one masterpiece based upon another. Boito, himself a composer, has reconstituted Shakespeare's play into a model libretto, losing nothing of importance on the way and heightening the drama by the tautness of his operatic framework. He abandons most of the first act and the opera opens without an overture in the middle of a storm at Cyprus, with an excited crowd watching Otello's ship battling through the high seas to safety. *Otello* begins with such force that on its first night one gentleman suffered a heart attack. This impetus is kept up until the fourth act where, without the jealous Otello's presence, there are twenty minutes of quiet lyricism from Desdemona who, awaiting death, sings her Willow Song and the Ave Maria. Elsewhere, despite peaceful goings-on upon the stage, we are always aware of Otello's brooding passion. This character is something quite new in Verdi's operas, and one whom the music holds up to be potent, dignified (until Act III), and finally sublime in a kind of transfiguration before his suicide.

Realising the kind of opera he was about to compose, Verdi always referred to it as 'the Chocolate Project' so as to put off the inevitable approaches from prominent singers to create his new characters. One can understand why Verdi considered calling the opera 'Iago', for this character is far more credible in the lyric theatre than he sometimes is otherwise. Music underlines his streak of insanity, together with his ingratiating manner, so that Otello is completely taken in by his pretended honesty, while we can see further into him than the

Bill of the première of Mozart's
Le Nozze di Figaro *at the*
Burgtheater, Vienna, on 1 May
1786

Below: Le Nozze di Figaro
with Geraint Evans and Teresa
Berganza. Covent Garden 1963

Moor can by listening to the orchestral comments. The opera becomes a 'two-handed' work, pointing the unnatural conflict between Iago and Otello, rather than between Otello and his wife Desdemona. She has, apart from the two numbers already mentioned, two beautiful duets with Otello, but as in the play it is a vapid character.

The only part of the first act of the play that has been preserved is from the Senate scene where Otello tells how he wooed and won Desdemona. It comes into the love duet at the end of Act I of the opera, as a kind of reminiscence between them. The only unauthentic piece of text is Iago's 'Creed' in which he affirms his atheism and exhibits his unbalanced mind. For the first time Verdi has achieved a through-composed opera, ceasing to depend upon a succession of arias and ensembles as hitherto, but in a fusion of these, all constructed in a powerful musical arc, well able to bear the strain of changing dramatic situations at any point. Herein lies the strength of *Otello* which shows Verdi moving one step nearer to his adversary Wagner in terms of the 'new music'.

Drawing of Tamagno and Maurel as Otello and Iago in the jealousy scene from the opera's première in Milan in 1887

Parsifal

Sacred festival drama by Richard Wagner in three acts with text by the composer. First performance Festspielhaus, Bayreuth, 26 July 1882.

This is a sacred opera about the triumph of Christianity over black magic, about redemption and salvation, the theme of all Wagner's operas. In this, his last work, he probably confesses his full acceptance of Christianity but certainly uses the second greatest story of all as a dramatic vehicle. (He was planning another about Jesus.) *Parsifal* was intended as a ritual, to be heard only at Bayreuth, and it was only through shortage of funds that the general public were ever admitted to it. Wagner had hoped to allow only a few specially chosen friends to share the experience of *Parsifal* with him. In listening to it now, as we are all able to do, it is difficult to understand the arguments about it being nothing but Nietzschean philosophy treated by Wagner merely because of its dramatico-musical possibilities. For evidence of his sincerity we have only to

Otakar Kraus as the evil magician, Klingsor in Parsifal. *This especially good make-up emphasises the singer's naturally protruding eyes and sharp features, to horrible effect*

listen to the music of the Grail scenes, to Gurnemantz's words, to Klingsor's utterances before his own destruction. To some people, including such composers as Delibes and Stravinsky, *Parsifal* is so unacceptable as to be positively obnoxious, yet this may reflect their own views of Christianity. For unlike *Der Ring* with its largely unrecognisable symbolic instruments derived from Norse mythology, Parsifal's symbolism is based on familiar objects and events: the Spear that pierced Christ's side, the Holy Grail used at the Last Supper, and a character based on Mary Magdalene.

The story tells how the evil magician Klingsor, once a Knight of the Grail but (like Satan) excluded from good so that he sinks to the depths of ill, caused Amfortas, King of the Knights, to be seduced by Kundry. Klingsor stole the Spear from him and pierced his side with it in an attempt to bring down the Order. Only Amfortas can conduct the ceremony of Communion with the Crystal Cup, which fortifies the knights for their quests. Unless Amfortas's wound is touched again by the same Spear it can never heal, and now Klingsor

has the Spear while Amfortas lives an agonising half-life. The only one who can hope to put things to rights is 'the pure fool, made wise by pity'. This is Parsifal, who at first fails completely to understand his mission. Eventually, he meets Kundry and Klingsor, the gorgeous Flower Maidens (humanised visions of voluptuousness), seizes the Spear, destroys Klingsor, converts and baptises Kundry and cures Amfortas by a touch of the Spear. He is then made King of the Knights of the Grail.

Wagner has advanced his compositional techniques even further than in *Tristan und Isolde* (q.v.) so that they begin to foreshadow Strauss's *Elektra* (q.v.), while his methods of condensing and expanding time and space in the opera are truly magical: mainly by transformation scenes between changes within each act. The most celebrated of these is the 'Good Friday Music', often played as an orchestral item outside the opera but intended to be the instruction of Parsifal in the Ritual of the Grail by old Gurnemantz, a Knight-elder who directly and indirectly helps Parsifal throughout the story.

Parsifal (Wagner). The curiously innocent youth, Parsifal (Vickers), surrounded by enticing Flower Maidens in Klingsor's castle

Pelléas et Mélisande

Lyric drama by Claude Debussy in five acts (twelve tableaux) with a text taken directly from Maurice Maeterlinck's drama. First performance Opéra Comique, Paris, 30 April 1902.

In the words of Edward Lockspeiser, Debussy's biographer, '*Pelléas* as a play is in fact an opera libretto in search of a composer'! It had to wait only ten years, but this demonstrates the perfect fit of words and music, of mood and atmosphere, of the fairy-tale whose mysticism Debussy matched to perfection. This composer has been the greatest single influence on his successors of all races, so it is strange that *Pelléas* has no operatic progeny, save perhaps in Delius's *A Village Romeo and Juliet*. At the same time *Pelléas* contains strong elements of Wagnerism, not least in the way the score holds the story aloft and links scenes with continuous music. This made Richard Strauss exclaim aloud at an early performance in Paris: 'But that's pure *Parsifal*!' By contrast Debussy has created the first symbolist opera by means of vague, suggestive outlines and repeated innuendos which echo the text. The score makes a continuously beautiful sound, often with divided strings and a general semblance of lightness, although it is interesting to note that it is identical to that required for *Tristan* save for one bass clarinet.

Debussy hardly alters Maeterlinck's story which opens in a forest where a weeping girl, Mélisande, is discovered alone. She is taken home by Golaud, grandson of old King Arkel. Golaud's letter, telling of his marriage to Mélisande, is addressed to his half-brother Pélleas, but read by their mother Geneviève. Pelléas has been described as 'so pale and feeble, and overcome by destiny'. Mélisande is seen playing with her wedding ring over a well, and when it falls in, Pelléas wants her to tell Golaud the truth, but she says she lost it in a grotto by the shore. Pelléas takes Mélisande there and they are frightened by three mysterious beggars. Pelléas passes Mélisande's window where she is combing her hair, and Golaud finds him caressing it. He insists that his brother leave Mélisande alone, and later when he suspects that Pelléas and Mélisande are together inside the castle, he holds up his small son Yniold (by a former marriage) who tells him that they are only sitting side by side in silence. Pelléas decides to leave the castle. Golaud drags Mélisande to the ground by her hair in a jealous rage. When she goes to say goodbye to Pelléas outside the gates they shut and she cannot get back inside. Golaud hunts for Pelléas in the undergrowth and kills him. Arkel, Golaud and a doctor stand round Mélisande's death-bed: she has had a tiny daughter. Golaud insists on questioning her continuously about her association with Pelléas until the servants all come in and kneel at the moment of Mélisande's death. She has never answered her husband.

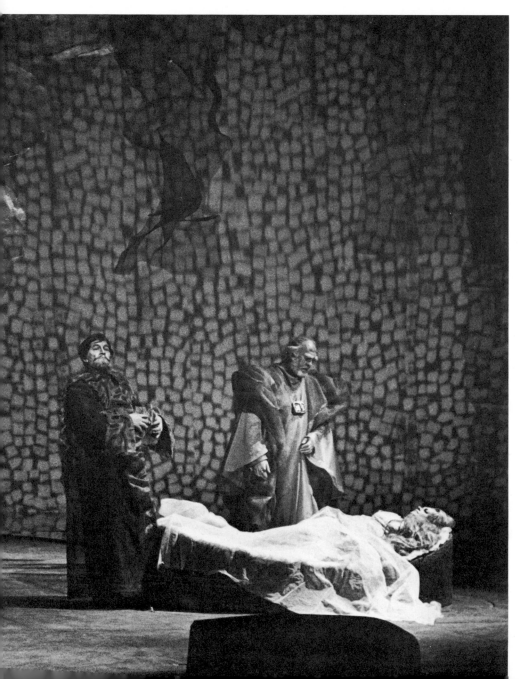

Peter Grimes

Opera by Benjamin Britten in three acts with a libretto by Montagu Slater after George Crabbe's poem 'The Borough'. First performance Sadler's Wells, London, 7 June 1945.

Peter Grimes marks a new stage in English opera, for it came at a time when England's, and Britain's, operatic endeavours were starting up again. It showed that there was again an opera composer worthy of continuing in the tradition of Purcell. Britten, who is so closely identified with the Suffolk coast, found this story irresistible and has given it a true flavour of East Anglia. The opera contains the first of his portrayals of characters who have been excluded from society for one reason or another. Peter Grimes, a fisherman, has lost a boy apprentice at sea under unusual circumstances. He attends the inquest and is acquitted on the understanding that he takes no more apprentices. All the townsfolk turn against Grimes except the schoolmistress, Ellen Orford, who helps him to find another boy. Peter behaves roughly to the boy and Ellen reproves him. They quarrel. It becomes known that Peter has taken the boy to his hut on the cliff, and all the villagers set out there in a mood of righteous

indignation. Peter and the boy try to avoid them by taking a steep cliff path to the beach, but the boy slips and falls to his death. Grimes is not found and does not turn up for three days. Then in the early morning, exhausted both mentally and physically, he consults Balstrode, a retired sea captain, who advises him to take his boat out to sea and sink with it. As the villagers get up for another daily round, Grimes has sailed out to sea and drowned himself.

Despite his conviction that opera is the most fascinating musical form, Britten was economically unable to write another on such a large scale as *Grimes* until *Billy Budd* in 1951; and after an output of altogether fifteen operas, *Grimes* remains the most satisfactory and successful of them all. The 'Four Sea Interludes' are often given as an orchestral piece in concerts, while the opera has been heard all over the world. Its tangy sea flavour, the skilful expressions of mood and innermost thought, in particular the tortured character of Peter contrasted with the humdrum personalities of the village, make it a most moving, tragic experience. An audience is bound to find this ordinary convention irresistible and the tangled person of Peter most arresting.

Der Rosenkavalier *(Strauss-Hofmannsthal). The Presentation of the Silver Rose Scene at Covent Garden in 1931 with Elisabeth Schumann as Sophie and Margit Angerer as Octavian*

Der Rosenkavalier

Comedy for music by Richard Strauss in three acts to a text by Hugo von Hofmannsthal. First performance Hofoper, Dresden, 26 January 1911.

Der Rosenkavalier is the supreme high comedy in opera. Hofmannsthal's setting and language of Vienna in *c.* 1745 with very true-to-life characters bear the mark of invention, although he took many names, phrases and incidents from a courtier's diary of the time. It is an opera of sexual rather than of spiritual love that accords well with the stereotyped conventions of the period. But there is nothing stereotyped about Strauss's score, indeed it makes great use – anachronistically – of the Viennese waltz. It is abundantly rich, vibrant with emotion and passion, and contains memorable tunes galore and one high-point of Strauss's composing achievement, the Presentation of the Silver Rose.

The story is about a noble lady, the Marschallin, who, still young, entertains lovers in her bedroom while her husband is away. At the start of the opera it is the young and idealistic Count Octavian who has spent the night with her, and

who is forced to put on a maid's clothes to prevent compromise when the gross and impoverished Baron Ochs bursts in to find why the Marschallin has not replied to his note asking her to nominate an envoy to carry his love-token. Ochs's vulgar advances to the 'maid' when he invites 'her' to supper are all brilliantly set by Strauss in a quick *parlando* manner as an aside to his supposed conversation with the Marschallin. Despite Octavian's warnings to her, the Marschallin proposes a certain Count Octavian to be the bearer of the Silver Rose. In Act II we meet Sophie, Ochs's bride-to-be, a young and inexperienced little madam, daughter of an immensely rich and recently ennobled parvenu, von Faninal. Sophie is repulsed by the sight of Ochs, while she and Octavian fall madly in love. Octavian is so frustrated by Ochs's appalling behaviour to Sophie that he picks a quarrel with the Baron and pinks him in a duel. Sophie declares that she will never marry the Baron, Octavian is shown the door and Faninal sees all his hopes of advancing Sophie being wrecked. In Act III, Octavian, again dressed as the maid 'Mariandl', meets Ochs by arrangement at a seedy inn, and proves a miserable and uncooperative guest. Various apparitions (planted there by Octavian) materialise in resemblance of Octavian –Mariandl who so bedevils Ochs. When a police commissar arrives to question the Baron he says that Mariandl is his fiancée, Sophie von Faninal. At that moment Sophie and her father arrive, Faninal has a mild heart attack and the Marschallin is summoned – accidentally, but providentially. She sizes up the whole situation at once, dismisses Ochs and his attempts at blackmail, soothes Faninal and yields Octavian to Sophie in the remarkable Trio. But the young couple's future happiness is in some question if we are to believe the cynical accompaniment to their love-duet.

The opera abounds in good humour, yet is tinged with sadness and seriousness, especially in the Marschallin's premonition of her losing Octavian and the sudden realisation that she has grown too old for him. Despite the apparent pastiche, all the underlying sentiments are – sometimes cruelly – real.

La Traviata

Opera by Giuseppe Verdi in three acts to a text by F. M. Piave after Alexandre Dumas *fils'* novel *La Dame aux Camélias*, based on incidents in his life. First performance Venice, La Fenice, 6 March 1853.

This opera was a failure at its first production, for three reasons. It was Verdi's first effort at freeing himself from the rigorous convention of Italian operatic style, and the audience did not understand his motives; it was performed in contemporary dress, and they felt cheated of sensational costumes; and the subject, a courtesan as heroine, offended public taste. But today *La Traviata* is performed more often than any other Verdi opera.

Violetta Valéry, a Parisian lady of easy virtue, meets Alfredo Germont at one of her parties. They are left together while the other guests are having supper, and Alfredo declares his love for her. For once she feels that a man might mean something to her, but shrugs off the idea with a laugh because she enjoys her own kind of life too much. All the same she goes to live with Alfredo outside Paris but has to sell her jewels to keep them. When Alfredo discovers this he goes to Paris to raise money and in his absence his father, Giorgio Germont, comes to ask Violetta to give up his son since her liaison with the family is seriously affecting Alfredo's sister's own marriage chances. Violetta sadly agrees, and Germont Père is greatly impressed by her dignified personality as well as moved by her sacrifice. The distraught Alfredo goes in search of Violetta, not knowing the reason for her disappearance. Some time later, when Violetta has taken up with an elderly Baron, she and Alfredo meet at another party. But he is indignant and rough with her, challenges the Baron to play for

La Traviata *(Verdi–Piave) at the Metropolitan Opera, New York, with Stuart Burrows as Alfredo and Beverly Sills as Violetta*

high stakes, and wins. He then insults Violetta before the whole company by throwing the money at her. Giorgio Germont unexpectedly arrives at this moment, reproves his son for his behaviour and publicly disowns him. In the last act Violetta is dying of consumption, and in her poverty-stricken little room she reads a letter from Alfredo's father, telling her that his son now knows everything and is coming to ask her pardon. A carnival procession goes by outside, cynically accentuating her own distress, but then Alfredo runs in, full of love for her again. She tries to dress to go away with him, but it is too late and she dies in his arms.

La Traviata goes to the heart of passion, anger, jealousy, forgiveness and all kinds of human love: fatherly, pure and immodest. The score is a masterpiece of mood and of clear insight into the characters' very thoughts and emotions, while the melodies are some of Verdi's greatest inspirations.

Tristan und Isolde

Opera by Richard Wagner in three acts to a text by the composer, after Celtic legends. First performance Munich, Court Theatre, 10 June 1865.

Wagner completed the score of his musically most revolutionary opera in 1859 after two years' work on libretto and music. Much of the inspiration came from his having fallen in love with Frau Wesendonck, on whose husband's estate he was staying. In 1861 he persuaded the Vienna Opera to produce the work, but after fifty-four rehearsals they abandoned *Tristan* as unplayable and unsingable. Not until 1865 was it performed, in Munich, thanks largely to King Ludwig II's patronage of Wagner. Its difficulties lay in the entirely new concepts which, in particular, the named protagonists' roles required. Many a performance has witnessed two, if not three different Tristans (one to an act) because the singers did not possess the vocal stamina to continue. Quite apart

from the physical demands upon singers, who have to carry the whole work through without the 'normal' assistance of a chorus, and the concentration of the drama upon a mere handful of artists, the required mental range is enormous, and the pitch to which Wagner drives his forces is sometimes almost unbearable. As a story it was once considered so objectionable as to be blasphemous, together with the 'wicked' score whose agonising harmonies and the ecstasy of the 'Tristan chord' made its general acceptance a slow business. It was not produced again until nine years after the première.

The story tells of Isolde, an Irish princess, who is being conducted to Mark, King of Cornwall, to be his bride, by the knight, Tristan. He refuses to speak to Isolde on board the ship which is taking them to Cornwall, except through his trusty henchman, Kurwenal. Isolde tells her companion, Brangäne, how Tristan slew her former fiancé to win her, and how she nursed him back to health. She orders a cup of poison to be prepared, but out of sympathy Brangäne substitutes a love potion. Tristan and Isolde drink it and become desperately, blindly in love with each other. In Act II, in Cornwall, they meet at night in the castle grounds when King Mark has supposedly gone hunting. Brangäne proves a poor sentry and the lovers are caught in the act by Mark and his courtier Melot who has not only betrayed Tristan, but now wounds him badly. In the last act, Tristan is in Brittany, slowly dying. His delirious visions of Isolde so exhaust him that he dies at the moment of her arrival. She falls, griefstricken, over Tristan's body, Kurwenal and Melot are killed, and the saddened King Mark declares that he would have given up Isolde to Tristan because of their great love. Isolde's *Liebestod* – or her panegyric upon her death through love – which concludes this marvellously wrought opera, is a microcosm of the whole work.

Tristan und Isolde *(Wagner). A most imaginative design for Act I on the ship bound for Cornwall. The vessel's design is distinctly un-nautical, but it creates a good effect and is utterly practical in operatic terms*

145

*Wozzeck (Berg). Above: The mad
Captain sung by Francis Egerton.
Right: Sir Geraint Evans as
Wozzeck menaces his woman,
Marie, played by Marie Collier*

*Far right: Announcement bill
first performance of* The Magic
Flute *at Covent Garden, for which
Her Majesty Queen Victoria has
given special permission for this
German opera to be performed
there, on 27 May 1833.*

Below right: Die Zauberflöte
*(Mozart–Schikaneder). Sheila
Armstrong as Pamina and Brian
Burrows as Monostatos.
Glyndebourne 1973*

Wozzeck

Opera by Alban Berg in three acts to a libretto by the composer after the play by
Büchner. First performance Berlin State Opera, 14 December 1925.

Each act of this powerful, episodic opera comprises a number of short scenes,
each self-contained, which propel the drama onwards faster and faster towards
its inevitable conclusion. The scene is set in a sleazy atmosphere where the
characters are made to appear mentally dirty as well. Wozzeck is a simple
soldier who lives with his mistress Marie and their son, and is the butt of two
older men, the eccentric army Captain, and the insane Doctor. In the first act,
Wozzeck is being teased by the Captain; he goes gathering sticks with his
friend Andres near the river, hears strange sounds and sees ominous shapes and
colours. Marie flirts with a Drum-Major from her window. Wozzeck has to
suffer an examination by the Doctor who is experimenting with his body. Marie
is gladly seduced by the Drum-Major. In Act II, Wozzeck's suspicions of Marie's
infidelity are aroused, especially when the Captain reaffirms them. Wozzeck

finds Marie dancing with the Drum-Major who boasts of his conquest and orders Wozzeck to drink with him. Wozzeck refuses and assaults him. In Act III, Marie is reading the Bible (the woman taken in adultery) as an act of repentance. Wozzeck takes her for a walk by a pond and stabs her. He goes to an inn where the company see blood on his hands. He runs back to the pond to find the knife, but drowns. Wozzeck's child is playing with other children and fails to understand what they mean when they tell him that his mother is dead.

Of course *Wozzeck* is a sordid work, and the score is in an unmelodious form called *Sprechstimme*, where the vocal line approximates only to the rise and fall of ordinary speech. There are no arias or set numbers, but, far from being haphazardly constructed, the opera is firmly based upon recognisable musical forms with each short scene representing one of them. It is easily followed and is most gripping in performance, while the style of musical presentation becomes acceptable the more it is heard. Its ugliness in portraying those vicious moments in the story are compensated for by the total result, which is that of a masterpiece. Berg uses a number of special effects in his orchestra, one of which is the 'unison burst' when every instrument takes up one note from soft to very loud until the whole opera house seems about to 'take off'. The second of these dissolves into a honkey-tonk piano in the inn on the stage. The only 'happy' scenes are those showing the illicit affair between Marie and the Drum-Major, which form fascinating contrasts with her moment of intense anguish as she reads the Bible.

Die Zauberflöte

Opera by Wolfgang Amadeus Mozart in two acts to a text by Emanuel Schikaneder from a play by Karl Ludwig Giesecke after the story 'Lulu' in Wieland's *Dschinnistan*. First performance Vienna, Theater auf der Wieden, 30 September 1791.

Despite its protracted sources, *Die Zauberflöte*, 'The Magic Flute', is an opera about love in its highest form, and of the overthrow of evil forces in the guise of women and Moors. Schikaneder and Mozart were both Freemasons, but the strong Masonic influence in the opera is no bar to an understanding of it. Essentially the story is a simple one, but it allows for every level of comprehension just as the plot is concerned with every level of humanity. It is a noble and high-minded story transformed into a parable with a profound message for all mankind. Mozart's score explains and underlines the story with great delicacy and with even greater musical simplicity, and with complete understanding and sympathy for the characters. The nobility and purity of Tamino and Pamina, the earthiness of Papageno, the temperamental outburst of the Queen of Night, the baseness of Monastatos, the godlike quality of Sarastro are each perfectly expressed in the music, by Mozart's genius.

An Eastern prince, Tamino, has been given a magic flute, and his appointed follower Papageno (a fantastic and feathered little man, a bird-catcher) has a set of magic bells. They are sent by the Queen of Night with these unusual gifts to rescue her daughter Pamina from Sarastro's Temple to which she has been abducted. Tamino has already fallen in love with Pamina from her portrait. The story seems to be a paradox by the end of the first act, for we do not know whether to believe the Queen of Night or Sarastro. When he realises that Sarastro is the embodiment of everything good and pure, Tamino is allowed to undergo trials of initiation into the higher life. Papageno follows him, although his trials are modified to suit his temperament. After suffering and despair he wins his little feathered wife, Papagena. Pamina, too, is led to attempt suicide because Tamino's vow of silence makes her think he does not love her; but she accompanies him on the last stage of his trials, and together they obtain a blessed union from Sarastro.

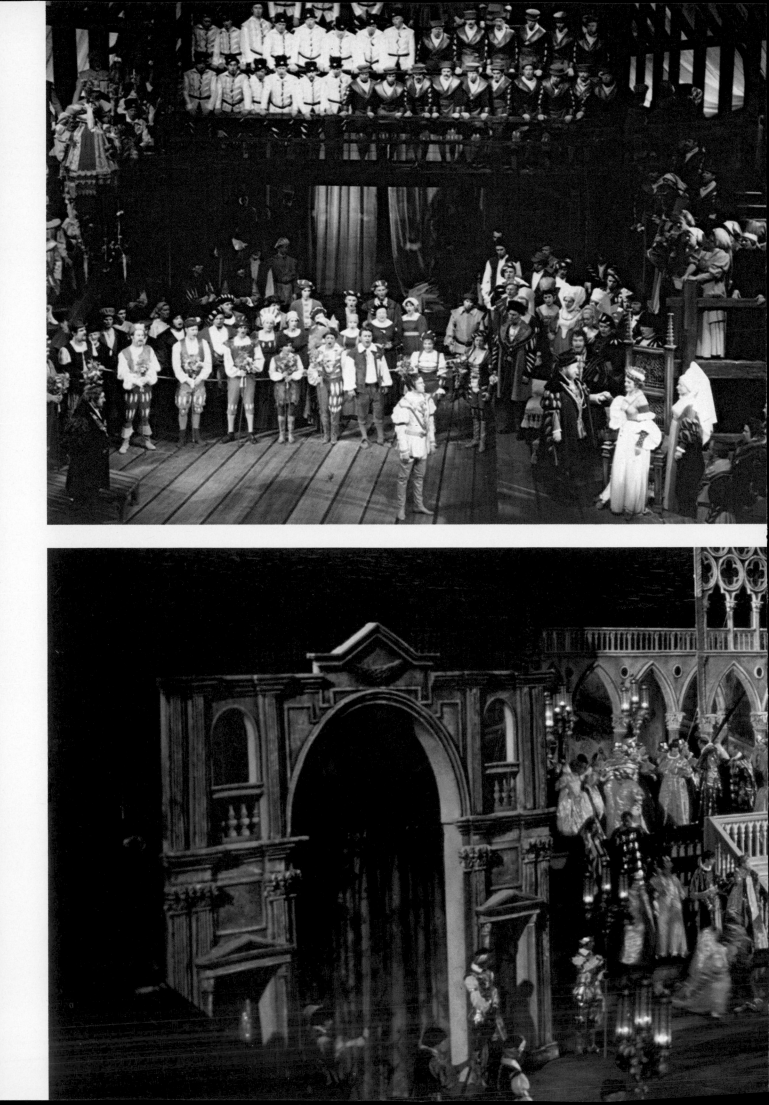

VII *Great Singers of the Twentieth Century*

*T*he American soprano Geraldine Farrar once said: 'When you wish to discuss singers there are two you must put aside. One is Caruso, the other is Rosa Ponselle. Then you may begin.' Thirty years later, Miss Farrar might well have included Maria Callas on her high pinnacle of choice, but in any form of art there can be only a select number of angels.

The choice of a handful of singers from among the thousands whose careers are famous, is not only a controversial matter, but a somewhat unenviable task. Consequently this selection is not an entirely personal one, because voices charm and delight in different ways and, after all, it is not necessarily the voice or the acting alone which determines star quality.

That there should be so many sopranos may seem unfair to the relatively few tenors, but then, there are so many more good soprano roles in opera.

Maria Callas

Maria Callas, the Greek-American soprano, was born Maria Kalogeropoulos in New York on 4 December 1923, and went to Athens in 1936. After exclusive study with the Spanish soprano, Elvira de Hidalgo, at the Athens Conservatoire, her professional début in 1945 was in Suppé's *Boccaccio*. Her Italian début was at Verona on 3 August 1947 as Laura in *La Gioconda* (singing opposite Richard Tucker), but then she began to study and sing Wagnerian roles alongside the heavily ornamented ones of Bellini and Donizetti. In 1949 she married the rich industrialist, Meneghini, and settled in Italy. Callas's London début as Norma in 1952 was a sell-out at all three performances, and she returned in 1953 to sing the same opera six times to packed houses. She was of ample proportions but soon began to slim so that her voice, never without its technical disadvantages of strained, pinched and off-pitch high notes as well as a pronounced tremolo towards the end of a performance, showed signs of early wear, partly as a result of its diminished physical support. But all this became of small account when Mme Callas appeared. She always studied her characterisation very carefully and *was* that character on the stage; likewise her keen intelligence was apparent, both in the opera house and through the recorded performance. She had the aura of a great person which, when coupled with her astonishingly powerful, expressive and generally beautiful voice, produced a devastating effect on audiences. Her scope was wider even than Rosa Ponselle's, and came nearer to Lilli Lehmann's in that she sang Isolde, Brünnhilde, Violetta and Lucia. Her temperamental outbursts, due to an unhappy private life, gave her advantageous publicity but made a number of managements chary about engaging her. Maria Callas's New York début as Norma on 29 October 1956 was the occasion for a heavy publicity campaign which had not been experienced there before in connection with an opera singer. Her last appearances were as Tosca in London and as Norma in Paris.

Mme Callas was obliged to give up her operatic career while still relatively young, although she undertook a concert tour with the tenor Giuseppe di Stefano in the early 1970s, with only piano accompaniment. These were pale shadows, vocally speaking, of her former glory. Those who heard her in her prime will argue that she is the greatest soprano-actress of this century. Her exceptional powers, coupled with a strength of personality and a dynamic acting ability, are partly reflected in the many long-playing discs she made. Mme Callas was not particularly tall but could look so on stage. She was dark with huge, black eyes and the smile which lit up her whole face, whether expressing adoration or simple fun. Her voice was large and very 'covered' in tone. Her ability to produce seamless runs and to decorate her vocal line with accuracy and effectiveness gave her the right to be described as one of the last *bel canto* singers. Her death in Paris on 16 September 1977 was a tragic loss.

Maria Callas as Tosca

Enrico Caruso as Dick Johnson (left) in La Fanciulla del West

Enrico Caruso

Caruso was, quite simply, the finest male singer, if not the most talented and expressive singer altogether, in living memory. He was born in Naples into a large and poor family on 25 February 1873 and died there on 2 August 1921. Within these 48½ years an operatic meteor enriched the world's experience. Caruso's outstandingly beautiful tenor voice, coupled with an effective intelligence as well as the desire – and ability – to improve his technique all the time, enabled him to sing a wide variety of Italian roles and a few French ones. He seldom attempted anything in the German repertoire (although he once sang some excerpts from *Tristan* to a group of friends), and was careful to ensure that his characterisation and diction were always perfect. He only ever essayed English on wartime records.

Caruso's career came in three parts. First his début in Naples in 1894 in a now forgotten opera by Morelli which at once promoted him to becoming the most sought-after of Italian tenors. This phase lasted until 1906, and during these years he sang with Melba, Tetrazzini and all the most fashionable sopranos, making his technique well-nigh perfect. Between 1908 and 1909 Caruso's voice began to alter and he was obliged to adapt his technique accordingly; from then on, with a richer and darker instrument, he continued to amaze and delight his audiences in Europe and North America. His seventeen years at the Metropolitan Opera between 1903 and 1920 included a number of world and American premières, and he sang some forty-two different roles there. His last appearance at the Met was as Elezear in Halévy's *La Juive* on Christmas Eve 1920.

Caruso was an amazingly cheerful and happy person; he loved to encourage and help other singers; he amused himself by sketching his colleagues at rehearsals, and was most generous. How he helped a young, unknown singer to become a star and to sing with him at her operatic début is told below under Rosa Ponselle. Caruso was a good businessman and had the sense to price himself out of any engagement which he considered to be unsuitable to his reputation and his career. He realised the importance of recordings earlier than most singers and put himself under contract to HMV (Victor) as early as 1902. His records brought the world a great deal of pleasure and himself a fortune of

Feodor Chaliapin

about half a million pounds. Indeed he may be said to have established recorded music, and its means of reproducing music, as a serious business, not merely a toy. Caruso's gay spirits and sheer enjoyment of life and of singing were reflected in his smart clothes and his ebullient behaviour. His intense fits of nerves before every performance caused him to smoke very heavily and this may have been the reason for his illness in New York in 1920 and his death soon afterwards. The two contenders for his mantle, Giovanni Martinelli and Beniamino Gigli, were each fine artists, but no tenor has ever come within a stage's width of Caruso.

Feodor Chaliapin

Chaliapin, the Russian bass, was born at Kazan on 11 February 1873 (a fortnight before Caruso). He came of peasant stock and received little education of any kind. His singing was, in a sense, natural, and so were his ways of projecting characters through his voice and body, both outsize. He seized his first chance in St Petersburg to sing with a private opera company and went with them on a tour in southern Russia. In 1892 he had voice training from a tenor called Usatow in Tiflis and made his proper début there in 1893 as Mephistopheles in Gounod's *Faust*. By 1899 he was singing with triumphant success in Moscow where talent scouts from La Scala heard him, and he was engaged for the 1901 season in Milan. He returned there in 1904 and this led to an engagement for the Metropolitan Opera in 1907. However, he was not successful in New York because his larger-than-life Russian characters of Ivan the Terrible, Boris Godunov and so on, were misunderstood as mere 'ham' by American audiences. He was later received there with enthusiasm, especially in *Don Quichotte* by Massenet.

Chaliapin was a leading member of Diaghilev's Opera Company which took Paris by storm in 1907 and onwards, and he made his London début at Drury Lane in 1913 as Boris. He had a gigantic voice and an awesome appearance, especially in the death-scene of Boris, which was terrifying. Many stories are told about how he stopped stage quarrels between his colleagues merely by showing himself: his very appearance was enough to subdue them. In later years he gave concerts when his eccentricities became emphasised to the extent of taking snuff in complete silence for more than a minute, keeping his (slightly despised) pianist and the audience waiting breathlessly. But stagehands loved him (a good sign) and used to refer to him as 'Charlie Pin'. He was not a good businessman but was always willing to 'have a go', often in the best artistic sense, but too often in less than the best financial one. He made a film of *Don Quichotte* (though with a score by Darius Milhaud this time) and it shows his fondness for wearing an exaggerated make-up and then – surprisingly – filling it. Chaliapin died in Paris on 12 April 1938.

Kirsten Flagstad

Kirsten Flagstad was born at Hamar, Norway, on 12 July 1895 of two professional musicians. Her voice was trained by Ellen Schytte-Jacobsen in Oslo where she made her operatic début as Nuri in *Tiefland* by d'Albert. After further training in Oslo and Stockholm, she was engaged as a soubrette at the Mayol Theatre in Oslo where she sang only in operetta. Between 1928 and 1932 she sang at the State Theatre in Göteborg and was then going to retire from the stage to devote more time to her family, when she was summoned to Bayreuth to sing Sieglinde. This secured her a contract for the Metropolitan Opera in 1935 where she sang Sieglinde, as well as her first Isolde and Kundry. This established her as a leading Wagnerian soprano alongside Frida Leider. In 1936, Kirsten Flagstad sang one cycle of *Der Ring* as well as four

Isoldes at Covent Garden, and returned in the following season. She continued to sing at the Metropolitan Opera until 1941, when she was unable to leave occupied Norway. Her husband, Henry Johansen, was a collaborator during the war, but Flagstad emerged unscathed from this connection and gave a sensational series of performances during a North American tour during 1947–8. She may be said to have revitalised interest in and acceptance of Wagner's operas in Britain immediately after the war when there was still a heavily unpleasant tang to them in many people's minds. In 1949 and 1950 she gave wonderful interpretations of Leonore in *Fidelio* at the Salzburg Festivals. She bade farewell to Covent Garden in 1951 with two cycles of *Der Ring*, an extra bonus as Sieglinde, Leonore in *Fidelio*, Kundry and five Isoldes. Later in that year she signed a comic contract with the actor Bernard Miles to sing Dido in Purcell's opera at a little theatre in Miles's garden called The Mermaid. Maggie Teyte (*q.v.*) sang Belinda. In 1952 she returned to the Metropolitan to sing Alceste, appeared in a Promenade Concert in London, and retired altogether in 1955.

Between 1958 and 1960 Mme Flagstad was a director of the Oslo Opera House and continued to make records, notably a complete *Tristan und Isolde* under Furtwängler, as well as parts of *Der Ring*. Fortunately she has left this legacy as to how she sang. Her exceedingly powerful, unshakeable, never-failing voice shone with great brilliance. Although it might sometimes have missed that extra bit of tonal warmth, it still possessed a great amount of warmth from the heart. Mme Flagstad was essentially a mother and a simple person. Most of her time between acts in the dressing-room was spent in knitting for her many grandchildren, about whom she talked with fond affection. She died in Oslo on 8 December 1962.

Tito Gobbi

Tito Gobbi was born at Bassano del Grappa near Venice on 24 October 1915. After beginning a legal career at the University of Padua, he took singing lessons with Giulio Crimi in Rome. He made his début in Rome on 27 June 1937 as Germont père in *La Traviata* (a young father indeed at the age of twenty-two) and in the following season he went to La Scala. In 1942 Gobbi created Wozzeck in the Italian première in Rome and continued to sing in Italy during the war. He first sang in North America at San Francisco in 1948 as Figaro in *Il Barbiere*, and made his Salzburg début as Don Giovanni on 27 August 1950. Later in that year he went to Covent Garden with the La Scala Company where he was first heard as Belcore in *L'Elisir d'Amore*, then as Ford in Verdi's *Falstaff*. As a principal baritone of world-wide fame in Italian opera, Tito Gobbi was much sought after, but did not go to the Metropolitan Opera until 1956 when he caused a sensation as Scarpia in *Tosca*. He sang this role with Maria Callas in London and Paris, and a film of Act II (abridged) was made at the time. His characterisations of Iago, Rodrigo (*Don Carlos*), Rigoletto and Don Giovanni have been acclaimed all over the world for their subtlety of interpretation. He is a consummate actor and since 1937 has made twenty-six films of opera.

Gobbi is a singer in the grand manner, has a fine and noble personality, and enjoys life to the full. His voice, occasionally apt to be a trifle dry, has stood up well to the test of time and of the 100 roles which he has interpreted, many of them more than a 100 times over. His make-up is a lesson in the craft; he is a stage designer and producer as well. His favourite part is Gianni Schicchi, for it gives him ample scope to indulge in humour of the kind he enjoys best, but he is especially fond of Puccini and Verdi. He sings only in Italian. He married Mathilde de Rensis, sister of Boris Christoff's wife, and he lives in Rome.

Hans Hotter

Hans Hotter was born at Offenbach-am-Main on 19 January 1909. From the age of seventeen he studied church music in Munich, played the organ and sang in a choir. In 1927 he studied singing with Matthäus Roemer (a de Reszke pupil) who developed Hotter's rich bass-baritone voice in a very short time. His début was at Troppau in 1930 and between 1932 and 1934 he was a member of the German Theatre in Prague. He then moved to Hamburg and three years later went to Munich, during the Krauss regime. He was to be heard both in Munich and in Vienna, especially in Wagner's operas. Hotter created the part of the Kommandant in *Friedenstag* in 1938, and that of the poet Olivier in *Capriccio* in 1942: both by Strauss and both in Munich. He was also a distinguished Jokanaan in *Salome* and Mandryka in *Arabella*. His début at Covent Garden was with the Vienna State Opera during their visit in 1947, as the Count in *Figaro* (in German). As a result of this visit, both he and the soprano Elisabeth Schwarzkopf were engaged to sing with the new British Opera Company in subsequent seasons. Hotter sang Hans Sachs (in English), Kurwenal and the *Walküre* Wotan in this season, then returned frequently until well into the 1960s, finally as a producer of *Der Ring*. In the fifteen years 1948–63 he was undoubtedly the most famous Wotan in the world, proclaiming himself the true follower of Friedrich Schorr. Hotter appeared regularly at the Metropolitan Opera between 1950 and 1954, while from 1952 he was engaged to sing Wotan-Wanderer and the Holländer at Bayreuth. During the late 1940s and 50s Hotter's performances in London were seriously impaired because they invariably took place in the summer, and the artist was a sufferer from hay fever. At other times of the year he was notable for his commanding presence, his very tall, dignified appearance, a Wotan without make-up.

Over the years his voice has grown darker, so that his farewell to the stage in Paris as Wotan in *Die Walküre* in 1972 was a different interpretation – as might be expected, intellectually – but also tonally different from his 1938 recording of Act II of this opera. Hotter still gives *Lieder* recitals – this has always been another facet to his singing art – and master classes. There is much still to be learnt from this man who has been singing consistently for the last forty-seven years.

Sena Jurináč

Sena Jurináč was born Sena Srebrenka in Travnik, Yugoslavia, on 24 October 1921. Her father was a doctor and her mother came from Vienna. She took up singing at the Zagreb Academy under Maria Kostrencič, and made her début in 1942 at the Zagreb Opera House as Mimi in *La Bohème*. In 1944 she became a member of the Vienna State Opera, where she sang Cherubino at her début and again in the first performance after the Opera House had been bombed. She accompanied the Vienna Company to London in 1947 and was first heard there as Dorabella in *Così*. Thereafter she was a regular singer at Glyndebourne and did not return to Covent Garden until 1959. She changed from Dorabella to

Hans Hotter as Wotan

Fiordiligi, from Donna Elvira to Donna Anna, but it is the ardent, excitable, impetuous, calf-loving boyish parts in which Mme Jurináč excelled in these years. Her Cherubino, Composer in *Ariadne*, Octavian in *Der Rosenkavalier* (all of which have been recorded and the latter filmed) were models of performing the roles: most beautifully sung and exquisitely acted. If she had done no more than these, her place in these pages would have been assured.

As her voice developed she began to assume more mature roles, such as a really delicate and perfect Madame Butterfly (with which she returned to Covent Garden), a thoroughly dramatic though somewhat puzzled Tosca (as if all the political events were beyond her), a really boyish Leonore in *Fidelio* whose courage and love for her husband shone through her performance, and then the Marschallin: only too well acquainted with the Octavians of this world, one might think. Her North American début was in 1959 in San Francisco, and she was first heard at Salzburg in 1947 as Dorabella, returning there often and playing Octavian in 1960 when the new Opera House was opened.

Sena Jurinač has a completely natural mode of vocal expression, a pure soprano voice with a good intelligence behind it. She can run the gamut of passions from anger and disdain to humour and pathos, and her appearance is still that of a young woman, belying her age. She is very beautiful. She was formerly married to the Italian baritone Sesto Bruscantini. Mme Jurinač is also a noted *Lieder* singer when all her stage attributes are channelled into this very personal and intimate branch of the art. But above all she is recognised as a very great interpreter of Mozart and Strauss.

Lotte Lehmann

Lotte Lehmann

Lotte Lehmann was born at Perleberg (Brandenburg) on 27 February 1888. She studied singing in Berlin with several teachers, completing her studies with Mathilde Mallinger. Then she joined the Hamburg Opera where she made her début in 1909 as the Third Boy in Mozart's *Die Zauberflöte*. In 1914 she sang Sophie in *Der Rosenkavalier* at Drury Lane Theatre, in Sir Joseph Beecham's opera season, once to Siems's and once to Hempel's Marschallin. In the same year she was called to Vienna and became one of the most beloved members of that company, assuming at once the character and personality of a Viennese and remaining one until 1938. In 1916, by default of another singer who did not turn up to a rehearsal, Lotte Lehmann was cast as the Composer in the revised version of *Ariadne* by Strauss. This led to her creation of another Strauss role, the Dyer's Wife in *Die Frau ohne Schatten*, also in Vienna, in 1919. In this she played opposite her operatic rival, Maria Jeritza, who sang the Empress. Owing to confused thinking at Covent Garden in 1924, where it was supposed that Lotte Lehmann either had sung or was singing the Marschallin in *Der Rosenkavalier*, she was asked to take this part, and agreed, although she had to learn it first. Her assumption of it became world famous: she *was* the Marschallin right up to her retirement. She is one of the few sopranos who has sung Sophie, Octavian and the Marschallin in this opera. She was the first Vienna Turandot in 1926, and in 1930 crossed the Atlantic for the first time to sing in Chicago. She was called to the Metropolitan Opera in 1934 when she sang Sieglinde to Melchior's Siegmund. This performance was recorded in Vienna. She created the first Vienna Suor Angelica and Arabella, and always a friend of Strauss, created the unique first Christine in *Intermezzo* in Dresden. Thereafter she sang Christine Storch only in Vienna, and another singer took over in Dresden. In 1938 she had to leave Europe, owing to political pressure, and became an American citizen. She continued to sing in the USA and to produce opera until 1945, when she devoted her considerable energies to teaching.

Mme Lehmann's last public concert was in 1951, but at her master classes in North America and in London she occasionally let a note slip, and we heard her again. These occasions will ever remain in the memories of those who attended them, for there she exhibited her extraordinary ability to project a role and a character before singing a note. She was a consummate actress and her voice and personality made her one of the warmest and most womanly sopranos of the twentieth century. She was always outspoken, and detested the second-rate in performances. She died in California on 26 August 1976.

Frida Leider

Frida Leider was born in Berlin on 18 April 1888. She worked in a bank and studied singing in her spare time, eventually taking to it full-time with Otto Schwarz in Berlin. She made her début in Halle as Venus in *Tannhäuser*, joined the Rostock Company in 1916, went to Königsberg and then to Hamburg between 1919 and 1923. She was then called by Max von Schillings to the Berlin State Opera, where she remained until 1940. Between 1924 and 1938 she appeared regularly in the summer seasons at Covent Garden as Brünnhilde, Senta, Donna Anna, Isolde, Kundry and the Marschallin, all tragical-heroic characters. She made her North American début at Chicago in 1932 as the *Walküre* Brünnhilde and first appeared at the Metropolitan Opera on 16 January 1933 as Isolde. Between 1928 and 1938 she sang Brünnhilde in the *Ring* cycles, Kundry and Isolde at Bayreuth. In the late 1930s she experienced great opposition in Germany because of her Jewish husband, the violinist Rudolf Deman. He fled to Switzerland and she remained in Berlin. After the war she gave only a few recitals, but became a producer and teacher at the Berlin State Opera. Between 1948 and 1958 she was a professor of voice at the Berlin Music High School, after which she remained there in retirement. Her voice was an extremely beautiful instrument, strong, reliable and well controlled, making her one of the foremost Wagnerian sopranos between the wars. Her performances were not only musically powerful but dramatically so, depending upon an extraordinary nobility and resignation. She died in Berlin on 3 June 1975.

Tiana Lemnitz

Tiana Lemnitz, daughter of a bandmaster, was born at Metz on 26 October 1897. She studied singing there and at Frankfurt-am-Main with Anton Kohmann, and made her début in 1920 at Aachen as Eva in *Die Meistersinger*. In 1928 she left for Hanover where she remained until 1933. Mme Lemnitz was then called to the Berlin State Opera where her first big success was as Elvira in *Ernani* under Leo Blech. In 1935 she was considered to be the best Octavian available, a role for which she was famous at Covent Garden in 1936 as well as Eva. In 1938 she sang Pamina in the famous recording of *Die Zauberflöte* in Berlin under Sir Thomas Beecham, and in the same year sang Elsa, Pamina and one performance of Sieglinde at Covent Garden. Although she was invited to sing at the Metropolitan in 1938 she declined the offer on political grounds because she identified herself with the regime in Germany. She remained at the Berlin Opera throughout the war where she sang many German and Russian roles, but always in German. Afterwards she lived in the eastern zone of Berlin, con-

Tiana Lemnitz as Octavian in Der Rosenkavalier

tinuing to sing (but the Marschallin instead of Octavian). In 1950 she made a surprise visit to the Teatro Colón in Buenos Aires to create Jenůfa for them, but otherwise did not go abroad. A movement to get her to sing again in London after the war did not succeed. Mme Lemnitz was one of the most beautiful sopranos between the wars, possessing great warmth and tenderness in her voice which also had an unmistakable quality. She made a great number of gramophone records all of which show her perfect technique and the ability to absorb each character differently, a style that was mature but never ripe, often with a gay youthfulness overriding everything else. As an actress, she was a past-master of subtlety and distinction. She now lives in West Berlin.

Richard Mayr

Richard Mayr was born on 18 November 1877 at Henndorf near Salzburg. While studying medicine at Vienna University he was persuaded by Gustav Mahler, in 1898, to have his voice trained. This he did at the Vienna Conservatoire, and was accepted into the Vienna Opera in 1902 as a bass-baritone. He remained a member for the rest of his life. His début at Bayreuth as Hagen in *Götterdämmerung* may seem today to be an unfamiliar kind of role for Mayr, but he

Richard Mayr as Baron Ochs

Lauritz Melchior

164

sang it there again in 1908, following that with a remarkably humane and lovable Gurnemanz between 1911 and 1914, and again in 1924. Mayr had also sung at two early Salzburg festivals, in 1906 and 1910, before they were properly established as we know them today. But with their foundation under the direction of Hofmannsthal, Reinhardt, Roller and Strauss, Mayr was called in for assistance, and in 1922 he sang Leporello at the first Salzburg Festival opera on 14 August, which Strauss conducted. Thereafter he sang Figaro (Mozart) Don Pasquale, Rocco in *Fidelio* (and one performance of Don Fernando), King Mark in *Tristan* and Sarastro, over the years until 1934. He caused a great sensation with his Dr Pandolfo (Uberto) in his production of *La Serva Padrona* in 1926.

It was Mayr's character as well as his ability to shine in comic roles which caused Hofmannsthal and Strauss to write the part of Baron Ochs with him in mind. But *Der Rosenkavalier* was to receive its première in Dresden, and Mayr belonged to Vienna. The director there, Felix Weingartner, who was not especially friendly towards Strauss, declined to release him. However, Mayr took the part for the Vienna première of the opera on 8 April 1911, thereafter making it his own. He was heard as Ochs on 21 May 1924 when he, Lotte Lehmann, Elisabeth Schumann and Delia Reinhardt were all making their Covent Garden débuts, and he continued to sing it there, unchallenged, until 1931. Mayr went to the Metropolitan Opera in 1927 for four seasons, making his début as Pogner in *Die Meistersinger*. Although there is ample proof on disc as to how he sang Ochs, it is unfortunate that no evidence exists of his Barak in Strauss's *Die Frau ohne Schatten*, a role he created at Vienna in 1919. Mayr was a true Austrian, beloved in Vienna and Salzburg, but inclined to be associated more with Baron Ochs than with any other interpretation. His rich bass voice could be turned with equal facility to more serious situations, for he was an excellent actor, an especially telling Gurnemanz. As a man he was a wonderful companion and thoroughly enjoyed life. He died in Vienna on 1 December 1935 and is buried at Salzburg. He sang only in German.

Lauritz Melchior

Lauritz Melchior was born Lebrecht Hommel in Copenhagen on 20 March 1890 (the same day as Beniamino Gigli). He studied with Paul Bang in Copenhagen and was first heard there in the baritone role of Silvio in *I Pagliacci* in 1913, and he continued to sing baritone roles until 1917. He was advised in London by the novelist Hugh Walpole, who heard him giving a recital, to consider becoming a tenor. He took this advice and relinquished the stage to study under Vilem Herold. In 1918 he emerged as a *Heldentenor* in *Tannhäuser*, but, still not content with his voice, he took further lessons during 1921-3 from four teachers, among whom were Anna Bahr-Mildenburg in Munich and Karl Kittel in Bayreuth. Melchior sang in every Covent Garden season but one between 1924 and 1939, when he portrayed Siegmund, Siegfried, Tristan, Lohengrin, Tannhäuser, Parsifal, Don Florestan in *Fidelio* and Otello (both in German and in Italian). He sang at Bayreuth between 1924 and 1931 and made his North American début at Chicago and San Francisco. He joined the Metropolitan Opera in 1926, when he sang *Tannhäuser* for his opening performance, and remained a member there until his retirement in 1950. He became an American citizen, turned to films and to lighter forms of singing, and also towards one idealistic ambition. This was to found an international school for *Heldentenors* which would have free exchange of students and currency. He visited a number of cities in Europe, attempting to raise funds, but although he was extremely welcome, the idea never succeeded.

Melchior's voice never seemed to tire or to age. This he ascribed to his training as a baritone and to the fact that only those who begin as baritones can ever

hope to withstand the rigours of the *Heldentenor* repertoire. He was a giant of a man, with the tenderness and sentimentality of the Copenhagener combined with a real desire to help future singers as much as he could. He died in Santa Monica, California, on 19 March 1974, one day before his eighty-fifth birthday, and with him passed the toughest male singer of the twentieth century.

Birgit Nilsson

Birgit Nilsson was born into a farming family in Karup, Sweden, on 17 May 1918. At first she decided to learn the farming business, but after some preliminary local training as a singer she went to the Royal Music Academy in Stockholm in 1941 and studied there under Joseph Hislop, a Scottish tenor long associated with Stockholm and with Covent Garden. In 1946 Mme Nilsson made her début in Stockholm as Agathe in *Der Freischütz* – as a soloist – and quickly added Lady Macbeth and the Marschallin to her accomplishments. In 1948 she began her Wagnerian career by singing Senta in *Der fliegende Holländer*, and scored a triumph as Donna Anna. Her first appearance in Britain was at Glyndebourne where, owing to the help and encouragement of Fritz Busch, she sang Elettra in *Idomeneo*, and began to develop her personality and to change her voice from the lyrical to the dramatic soprano. This proved excellent advice, for with her Salome and Brünnhilde in Munich she began her international career. Although she began her Bayreuth career with Elsa in *Lohengrin*, in 1954, she soon found her niche as Brünnhilde and Isolde there and at the major opera houses of Europe. It was at first inevitable that the Covent Garden audience should not take quickly to Birgit Nilsson so soon after the departure of Kirsten Flagstad, but before long she was as welcome in Floral Street as her Scandinavian colleague had been before her, and seats to hear her were at a premium also. In 1953 she sang Sieglinde, Elsa, Tosca, Aida and Amelia (*Ballo*) at the Vienna State Opera and in 1956 she gave guest appearances at San Francisco and Chicago. Her début at the Metropolitan Opera was in 1959 as Isolde. Her career is world-wide and her voice remains firm and unshakeable in spite of the amount of singing she does.

Birgit Nilsson is of formidable appearance and personality, and her pure and strong voice allows her to triumph equally in the Italian repertoire (provided the male voices are able to match hers) and in Wagner and Strauss. She has recorded the first uncut *Elektra* (previously considered unsingable) at one end of the scale, and *Turandot* at the other: a remarkable achievement. She lives in Zürich, is married to a Swedish veterinary surgeon and travels a good deal.

Luciano Pavarotti

Luciano Pavarotti has succeeded, against many odds, in becoming one of today's outstanding operatic tenors, a notable achievement when contrasted with others who seem to have reached the heights with ease.

Born in Modena, Northern Italy, on 12 October 1935, the son of a baker who was also a tenor, Pavarotti had the same wet-nurse as a soprano also born in Modena eight months earlier – Mirella Freni. 'It's obvious', she says, 'who got all the milk!' His size was not always against him, especially when he played football as a boy, and when he began to study singing seriously it was a distinct advantage. A pat on the head from Beniamino Gigli convinced Pavarotti of his destiny, and in 1961 he won the international singing competition at Reggio Emilia and sang his first Rodolfo in *La Bohème* under the famous conductor Molinari-Pradelli. This was followed by the Duke in *Rigoletto* at Carpi.

To sing such important roles in a land of singers at small opera houses means far less than it might do in other European countries. Pavarotti was partly successful in 1961, but he was stuck. He had fortunately attracted the interest of an artists' agent who got him an engagement for two weeks in Dublin, where they have an opera festival every year with most of the principal roles sung by Italians. One night Pavarotti was singing the Duke in *Rigoletto* and singing him extremely well. Joan Ingpen, casting director from Covent Garden, was there on the lookout for a promising young tenor to 'cover' the somewhat erratic Giuseppe di Stefano in some London performances of *La Bohème*. She was amazed at Pavarotti's voice and instantly engaged him for the possible emergency. The emergency happened and Pavarotti found himself singing three performances of Rodolfo in front of an excited and thrilled Covent Garden.

Now Fate lent a helping hand. Joan Sutherland and her husband Richard Bonynge had planned an operatic tour of Australia (with a short stop-off in Miami) but had no tenor. Most tenors are on the short side and Dame Joan is taller than most sopranos, so they were delighted and relieved when they encountered Pavarotti. They had found their tenor! Admittedly his vocal technique needed stabilisation and his acting required polish, but he already sang the roles they wanted and his opening *Lucia* opposite Dame Joan in Miami (his first performance in the USA) was prelude to a frantically successful reception in Australia. The joint recording programme for Decca–London records of Sutherland–Pavarotti–Bonynge stems from these years and continues as evidence of the well-applied faith they had in each other.

Pavarotti's tenor solo in the Verdi Requiem under von Karajan at La Scala in 1967 was his most prestigious engagement so far, and was not only the prelude to his La Scala début as Des Grieux in Massenet's *Manon* in 1969, but to his assumption of importance in the USA. The San Francisco Opera was the first leading house to welcome him, and he has since sung his début performances of seven leading Italian roles there.

While performing in *La Bohème* in San Francisco opposite Mirella Freni, Pavarotti was signed up by Sir Rudolf Bing for the Met, that goal of all singers the world over. He managed the first performance while suffering from influenza: a triumph of vocal technique as well as of mental and physical stamina.

The tenor roles in Bellini's and Donizetti's operas are nowadays difficult to cast, but Pavarotti's voice excels in this florid music. He is highly successful in the evergreen *Cav.* and *Pag.*; and he tackles the often cruelly high *tessitura* in Puccini's five main tenor roles with remarkable ease. The Italian Tenor's appearance in *Der Rosenkavalier* is a cameo that few leading tenors bother with, but in taking this very brief role on stage and on record, Pavarotti has shown what can be done with it. Joan Sutherland once persuaded him to sing Tonio in Donizetti's *La Fille du Régiment* in French – and what an incomparable event that was! – but generally speaking it is *Italian*, especially to the rarer *Gioconda*, *Amico Fritz* and *Guglielmo Tell*.

Pavarotti has recorded over thirty leading operatic roles in complete performances, has made many recital discs and has appeared to millions on television. He has done much to make the operatic tenor an approachable, popular and well-loved figure by his own warmth, humour and open friendliness, for he is not only an outsize man, but he possesses an outsize nature. Who else could invade the pop 'scene' with T-shirts that proclaim 'I love . . . . . . *Pavarotti*'?

His voice is an exceptional one: open in the Italian manner, bright as well as strong, and very incisive at the top. His LP: 'King of the High C's' makes no false claim, and the fact that he performs and records only music in the Italian tradition is kind to his astonishing voice. It will assist in preserving it to delight us for many years more.

Ezio Pinza

Ezio Pinza was born Ezio Fortunio in Rome on 18 May 1892. He wanted to be a racing cyclist, but changed his mind and studied singing at the Conservatoires of Ravenna and Bologna. His début was in 1914 at Spezia as Oroveso in *Norma*, an indication that his voice had always been bass and had started with that Italian bonus of quality. He was unable to continue his career during the First World War and served in the Italian Army until 1919. He returned to sing at the Teatro Verdi in Florence, and then made his Rome début as King Mark in *Tristan e Isolde* in 1921. In the same year he was called to La Scala and stayed there as principal bass, achieving enormous success during Toscanini's regime. Pinza went to the Metropolitan Opera in 1926 where he delighted his first-night audience as the High Priest in Spontini's *La Vestale* with Rosa Ponselle. He remained there as first principal bass in the Italian repertoire until 1948, singing Fiesco in the North American première of *Simone Boccanegra* in 1932. He did not go to Covent Garden until 1930, where he was first heard as Oroveso in *Norma* (again with Ponselle) on 26 May. He was a regular performer there until 1939, as well as in Paris and Vienna. He was introduced to Salzburg by Bruno Walter in 1934, where he sang Don Giovanni, Figaro (Mozart) and Don Basilio in *Il Barbiere*. During the Second World War, Pinza frequently appeared at the San Francisco Opera, singing a large number of roles, always in Italian – even Boris Godunov. In 1948 he retired from the opera stage and went into Broadway musicals, first in *South Pacific*, then in *Fanny*. He also appeared in films. He had a repertoire of about eighty operas and sang in fifty of them during his years at the Met. He was tall, dark and dashingly handsome with a flashing smile and a very likeable personality, which admirably suited him to play Don Giovanni. This he sang more than 200 times. His warm, luxurious bass voice had an unmistakable timbre and his portrayal of noble and tortured characters was only equalled in dramatic terms by his enormous sense of fun and zest in playing comic ones. He died in Stamford, Connecticut, on 9 May 1957.

Rosa Ponselle

Rosa Ponselle was born Rosa Ponzillo to immigrant Neapolitan parents who had a grocery and bakery business in Meriden, Connecticut, on 22 January 1897. She sang with her elder sister, Carmela, in cinemas and then in cabarets in an act called the Ponzillo Sisters. Rosa went for singing lessons with the impresario and vocal coach William Thorner, who had been a valet to Jean de Reszke. He was so impressed with her voice that he arranged for Caruso to hear her. Being fellow Neapolitans there was an instant bond, and the great tenor agreed with Thorner that the voice was quite exceptional. In the spring of 1918, when Caruso first heard Ponselle, the manager of the Metropolitan Opera, Gatti-Casazza, was trying to cast the Leonore in a production of Verdi's *La Forza del Destino*. No European sopranos were available because the war was still on, and it was then that Caruso suggested Rosa Ponzillo. After considerable doubt and argument, Gatti-Casazza agreed to audition the girl. She greatly impressed him, but he told her to go away and learn Norma's scena 'Casta Diva' and Leonore's aria 'Pace, mio Dio'. Ten days later she returned and sang them, and was accepted. She learnt the role of Leonore in five months and on 15 November 1918 she appeared with Caruso on the stage at the Met in that theatre's première of the Verdi opera.

Her success was instantaneous and she remained *prima donna* at the Met until 1937. She sang Rachel opposite Caruso in *La Juive* in 1919, Elisabeth de Valois in *Don Carlos* in 1920, and in 1925 Giulia in Spontini's *La Vestale*. It was not until 16 November 1927 that she sang Norma there. This was the opera with which she received the greatest applause of the season when she made her

Rosa Ponselle as Violetta

Below: Leontyne Price

début at Covent Garden on 28 May 1929. Her style of singing, her shadings of expression and her purity of tone, whether in quiet or dramatic passages, were considered remarkable. In the next summer season in London, Ponselle sang the first Violetta of her career, opposite Gigli, on 13 June. Great as the Italian tenor was, he paled by comparison with her, and nobody could remember having heard a better Violetta anywhere. In 1931 Ponselle appeared for the last time at Covent Garden in that theatre's first production of *Forza* on 1 June, conducted by Tullio Serafin, and she repeated her matchless *Traviata*. She never returned to London, nor did she ever sing at Salzburg. Her only other engagement outside America was for three performances of *La Vestale* at the Florence Maggio Musicale in 1933, otherwise she sang only in the USA. Rosa Ponselle sang twenty-one roles altogether at the Metropolitan Opera. She was always very nervous and had to summon up courage even to enter the house before a performance. Her last appearance there was a concert on 14 March 1937. Her last public concert was for Dwight D. Eisenhower's presidential election campaign in Baltimore on 5 October 1952.

Rosa Ponselle was one of the last true exponents of *bel canto*, for she was a *complete* singer. Furthermore she 'opened the doors of the Met' to American singers and serves as a shining example of how to succeed by persistence and confidence in one's art, however humbly it may have to start. When Lotte Lehmann asked Geraldine Farrar how Rosa Ponselle managed to have such a voice, she replied 'By special arrangement with God!' Rosa Ponselle lived in Baltimore until her death on 25 May 1981.

Leontyne Price

Leontyne Price was born in Laurel, Mississippi, on 10 February 1927. She studied voice at the Juillard School of Music and later in New York with Florence Page Kimball. Her concert début in 1950 led to her being cast in Virgil Thomson's *4 Saints in 3 Acts* in the 1951 revival in New York. She then joined an all-Negro cast and sang Bess in the two-year tour in Europe and Russia of Gershwin's *Porgy and Bess* opposite William Warfield, whom she married. They visited all the major cities between London and Moscow from 1952 to 1954 and were a great success wherever they played. In 1954 Leontyne Price gave a concert at the New York Town Hall and sang her first Aida at Chicago. This was repeated at San Francisco where she created the part of Mme Lidoine in the US première of Poulenc's *Les Dialogues des Carmelites*. For several years she was undoubtedly the finest Aida available, singing her at La Scala, Verona, Vienna, Covent Garden, the Städtischen Oper Berlin, and elsewhere. She was first heard at Salzburg in 1959 as the soprano soloist in Beethoven's Mass in D under Herbert von Karajan, and made her stage début there in the following season as Donna Anna. She returned to Salzburg in the same role in 1961, and sang Leonora (*Trovatore*) there in 1962 and again in 1963, always directed by von Karajan. Met audiences first welcomed Leontyne Price as Leonora in *Il Trovatore* in 1960, since when she has been a guest artist there. In 1966 she created the part of Cleopatra in Samuel Barber's *Antony and Cleopatra*, specially commissioned to open the new Met in the Lincoln Center. Miss Price has recorded many leading soprano roles, of which her Tosca is most notable.

Friedrich Schorr

Friedrich Schorr was born on 2 September 1888 at Nagyvárad, Hungary. He abandoned his intended career as a lawyer and studied singing with Adolf Robinson in Brünn and made his début as a bass-baritone in Graz as Wotan in *Die Walküre*. From this moment he began to grow in stature in the role until he became regarded as *the* Wotan of the 1920s and 30s. He remained at Graz until 1916 and then joined the German Opera in Prague for two years. After that he was at Cologne during Klemperer's regime and from 1923 to 1933 was a guest principal bass-baritone at the Berlin State Opera and in Vienna. In 1923 he toured North America with the 'German Grand Opera Company' and made his début at the Met as Wolfram in *Tannhäuser*. He remained a member of the company until 1943. Schorr sang at Bayreuth for five seasons between 1925 and 1931, singing Wotan-Wanderer in *Der Ring*. He was first heard at Covent Garden in 1924 when he made his début as Wotan in *Das Rheingold* on 5 May, conducted by Bruno Walter; and in later years he sang an admirable and poignant Holländer, a classic Hans Sachs, and one performance as Wolfram (*Tannhäuser*). In 1933 he was heard there for the last time in an inspired characterisation of Gunther in *Götterdämmerung*. In 1932, when opera at Covent Garden looked like coming to an end because of severe financial stress,

Elisabeth Schumann; Friedrich Schorr as Hans Sachs

Schorr was instrumental in persuading some of his German colleagues, notably Lotte Lehmann, Frida Leider, Lauritz Melchior and Herbert Janssen, to accept lower salaries in order to help the organisation to keep going. But in 1934 he and several other singers were so insulted at the cut-price offers for their engagement that season from Covent Garden's 'fixer', Otto Erhardt, that he never went back. Schorr continued to sing at the Met and throughout North America until 1943. His Pizarro in *Fidelio* was spine-chilling in its venomous intensity, while his creation of Daniello in the US première of Křenek's *Johnny Spielt Auf*, the first jazz opera, in 1929, and as Schwanda, also at the Met, showed his versatility. There was a single performance of *Die Walküre* at San Francisco in 1940 in which Lotte Lehmann sang Sieglinde, Flagstad sang Brünnhilde and Schorr sang Wotan. Act II has been preserved, and although it shows Schorr's voice in less good shape than on commercial recordings, he was still the darling of the audience. One of the great features of his voice was his ability to shade it from the towering rages of Wotan to the pensive and fragrant *mezza voce* of Hans Sachs. He was a fine, commanding actor, and his voice added to his visual authority. He continued to give *Lieder* recitals and to teach singing at the City Centre and in Manhattan. He then had his own school in Hartford, Connecticut, for opera singers. He died at Farmington on 14 August 1953, one of the few really great Wagnerian bass-baritones of his generation.

Elisabeth Schumann

Elisabeth Schumann was born on 13 June 1888 at Merseburg in Thuringia. She studied singing at Dresden, Berlin and Hamburg, and made her début at Hamburg as the Shepherd Boy in *Tannhäuser* in 1909. She remained there for the next ten years until she was called to Vienna where she was one of their most beloved sopranos, especially distinguished for her singing of Mozart. In the autumn and winter of 1921-2, Elisabeth Schumann and Richard Strauss under-

Margarethe Siems

took a long recital tour in North America when he accompanied her at the piano in seventeen cities, ending in New York. As a result she appeared in the first operatic season at Salzburg in 1922: as Despina in *Così* (conducted by Strauss), as Susanna in *Figaro* and as Blondchen in *Die Entführung*. She was a member of the Met Company between 1914 and 1915 and first appeared at Covent Garden in 1924 as Sophie in *Der Rosenkavalier* with Lotte Lehmann and Richard Mayr. In this season she also sang the Composer in *Ariadne auf Naxos*, and added, in later years, Eva, Susanna, Blondchen, Zerlina and in 1930 Adèle in the stunning production of *Die Fledermaus* with Lotte Lehmann, Maria Olczewska and Gerhard Hüsch, conducted by Bruno Walter. It was the first time that such a 'light' work had broken into the Royal Opera House and it was rapturously received. After 1933, like Friedrich Schorr and a number of other singers, she never returned there. When the Nazis entered Vienna in 1938, Elisabeth Schumann left and went to the USA. She taught singing at the Curtis Institute and continued, from time to time, to sing *Lieder*. At the 1946 Edinburgh Festival she returned, accompanied by Gerald Moore, singing with as much purity and silvery tone as ever before, and at the age of sixty-one. She was at one time married to the conductor, Karl Alwin.

Mme Schumann's Sophie has never been rivalled for the way in which she sang and acted the character, nor have her soubretteish Mozartean characterisations been taken with such dash and perfect style of singing. Her wonderfully warm personality and her kindness and attention to the needs of young singers, her attitude to her colleagues and the affection which she earned from them and from her audiences make her one of the most attractive and beloved singers of this century. She died in New York on 23 April 1952.

Margarethe Siems

Margarethe Siems was born on 13 December 1879 in Breslau (now Wroclaw) and studied singing in Dresden with Aglaja von Orgeni, who had been a pupil of Pauline Viardot and Mathilde Marchesi, and so learnt her art in the grand manner. Later she went to Mattia Battistini in Milan. Mme Siems made her début at the German Theatre in Prague in 1902 and remained there until 1908 when she was called to Dresden, then in its heyday under Ernst von Schuch. Between 1909 and 1912 she sang in three world premières of Strauss operas: as Chrysothemis in *Elektra*, as the Marschallin in *Der Rosenkavalier* (both at Dresden), and as Zerbinetta in *Ariadne auf Naxos*, with the play, at Stuttgart. Strauss had her rare voice in mind when composing the exceedingly taxing centrepiece scena for Zerbinetta, an aria which had later to be drastically simplified. Before the First World War, Mme Siems was a guest in London where she sang only the Marschallin at Covent Garden and Drury Lane; also in Berlin, Milan, St Petersburg and Amsterdam. She never left Europe and her career ended relatively early in 1920, after which she taught singing in Berlin, although she sometimes gave guest performances there and at Dresden where she settled in 1926. In 1937 she became professor of singing at the Breslau Conservatoire but returned finally to Dresden in 1946.

Apart from the roles mentioned above, for which she was especially famous, Mme Siems also sang Norma, Amina (*La Sonnambula*) and the Donizetti coloratura parts; Aida, Amelia (*Ballo*), Venus in *Tannhäuser* and Isolde. There had not been a voice like hers since Lilli Lehmann, trained in the Garcia *bel canto* tradition, enabling her to sing anything at all. This was emphasised by such opposite characters and roles as the Marschallin and Zerbinetta. Her appearance was autocratic but she had a good sense of fun. She was able to invest a tragic role with real tragedy and her Isolde possessed nobility and yearning pathos. She died at Dresden on 13 May 1952.

173

Placido Domingo

Among the leading tenors of today, Placido Domingo is unique. He has accomplished so much more than any other since Caruso, and his repertoire is wider than any since Jean de Reszke's. Placido Domingo ('Peaceful Sunday') was born in Madrid on 21 January 1941. His parents were celebrated Zarzuela artists, very much of the theatre, and in 1949 they all moved to Mexico to establish their own company, performing Zarzuelas and American Musicals in Spanish. The young Domingo made his stage début there whilst a student of conducting at the Mexico City Conservatoire: singing was a natural process for him. His operatic début was in *La Traviata* at the Mexico City Opera in 1961 where he sang several minor rôles before joining the Hebrew National Opera in Tel Aviv in 1962. Here he greatly developed his vocal technique and widened his repertoire. In 1965 he sang leading rôles in several North American cities before being called to the New York City Opera in 1966. His remarkable performances in three Donizetti operas, and in Ginastera's *Don Rodrigo* (which opened the New York State Theatre at the Lincoln Center Plaza) secured his 1968 début at the Met in *Adriana Lecouvreur*. This success placed him firmly as a principal tenor in great demand worldwide.

His British début was in Wales, at the 1968 Llangollen International Festival, soon followed by a Verdi Requiem under Giulini at the Royal Festival Hall. His Covent Garden début as Cavaradossi in *Tosca* ensured his recall there whenever possible, and his many successes have ranged from Don José to Otello. Although Placido Domingo's stage performances have embraced the wide span from Otello to Walther von Stolzing, he still wants to sing Tristan. His many recordings – the complete operas alone are getting on for fifty – and the videos, show his importance in the lives of musical people today. His perfectly controlled and beautiful voice that ranges from a golden top to a burnished copper lower register is not his only asset: his music is his birthright, he is an

Placido Domingo as Dick Johnson in La Fanciulla del West

experienced and persuasive actor, and with a winning appearance and infallible memory, what more could any artist want?

As well as being a kind and generous man, fond of young people, attentive to their needs and willing to sing their kind of music, his ambition to conduct opera has already been realised. For him this is as important as his singing and will become increasingly more so when, as his second career, Maestro Domingo will be guiding others from the benefit of his own experience as one of the greatest operatic tenors of the century.

Mariano Stabile as Iago

Mariano Stabile

Mariano Stabile was born at Palermo on 12 May 1888. He learnt with the great baritone and most famous singing teacher of his time, Antonio Cotogni, at the Santa Cecilia in Rome, and then made his début in Palermo as Marcello in *La Bohème* in 1911. Between then and 1922, Stabile built up a large repertoire of baritone roles (it eventually reached about sixty) and sang very conscientiously throughout Italy. When Toscanini returned to La Scala for his third term of office there in 1921, the first season opened with Stabile as Falstaff, a role with which he was especially associated for the rest of his life. Stabile became much sought after, following his association with Toscanini, and in 1926 he made his début at Covent Garden as Iago with Zenatello as Otello and Lotte Lehmann as Desdemona. In that season he also sang Don Giovanni and Falstaff. In the following years up to 1931 he added Marcello, Rigoletto, Scarpia, Gianni Schicchi and Gérard (*Andréa Chénier*) to his London repertoire. He never appeared at the Met, but his North American début was at Chicago in 1928-9 and he later went to Buenos Aires and sang at the Colón. He was a great favourite in the Italian repertoire at Salzburg from 1931, where he was first heard as Figaro (Rossini) and as Doctor Malatesta (*Don Pasquale*). Up to 1938 at Salzburg he also included Falstaff and Mozart's Figaro. Between 1936 and 1939 he was heard at Glyndebourne, and appeared at the Edinburgh Festival after the Second World War in 1948. Between 1946 and 1948 he was a member of Jay Pomeroy's Opera Company in London at the Cambridge and Stoll theatres where a new generation of opera-goers delighted in his Scarpia, Don Giovanni, Doctor Malatesta and, of course, Falstaff. In 1955 he sang opposite Maria Callas in Rossini's *Il Turco in Italia* at La Scala, and finished his career with a performance of Falstaff in Finland in 1963.

Stabile's voice, as a voice alone, was a true baritone with very good high notes, but not especially remarkable. It was his ability to combine his best vocal attributes with an all-round acting performance embracing great finesse in delivery which marks him as a thoroughly exceptional singing-actor. Furthermore, his training and the care with which he used his voice enabled him to go on singing the same major roles until he was over seventy. His wonderfully robust humour in Falstaff; his sardonic self-satisfaction as Baron Scarpia; his over-confidence and careless, though neat, treatment of others in an aristocratic impersonation of Don Giovanni (quite different from Pinza's – and they alternated in the years 1935–1937 at Salzburg); his ludicrous antics as Malatesta; and his lovely, pointed, scheming Figaro in Mozart's opera were each and all lessons in how to get the most out of the score and the libretto. Stabile used to watch the conductor very carefully, but this had the added advantage of enabling the audience to see his face and his eyes, which consistently gave a greater contact with him and a stronger reading into what he was up to. He was a master of the interpolated laugh, snort, exclamation in the vocal line which, far from interrupting it or coming as any sort of intrusion, added greatly to the feeling of the moment. His portrayals were thus more individualistic and complete than those of any of his contemporaries.

Conchita Supervia

Conchita Supervia

Conchita Supervia was born in Barcelona on 9 December 1895. She came from an old Andalusian family. At the age of thirteen she began to study voice at the Barcelona Academy of Music, and when only fifteen she made her début at the Colón, Buenos Aires, in a little-known opera by Tomás Bretón called *Los amantes de Teruel*. Only a month later she was heard at the same house in the supporting role of Lola in *Cavalleria Rusticana*. She followed this swift development with Octavian in the Rome première of Strauss's *Il Cavaliere della Rosa*, then went back to America and sang at the opera in Havana in 1914. For the 1915–16 season Supervia was in Chicago, and after the war she was to be found in the principal Italian opera houses and in Barcelona. She was called to La Scala in 1924 and in 1929 was their first Conception in the Scala première of Ravel's *L'Heure Espagnol*. In 1925 she sang in Turin where Vittorio Gui was anxious to revive some neglected Rossini operas requiring a coloratura mezzo-soprano voice. Supervia was ideally suited to this, and her *Cenerentola, Il Barbiere* (in the original version) and *L'Italiana in Algeri* were the result. She had also been singing Carmen since about 1912, a novel and very original interpretation of which seven numbers were recorded and explain her ideas of the gypsy girl. It is a thoroughly vivid and merry performance, bubbling with good nature, and sounding as if she had no intention of taking any man at all seriously. When she sang it in London, it was regarded by some people as outrageously idiomatic. Her engagement at Covent Garden was fraught with mischievous difficulties on Supervia's part. She would not sing Carmen before Cenerentola, and she would not rehearse Carmen after performances of Cenerentola had started. This Gilbertian impasse was resolved (although Supervia sued the Royal Opera House when they cancelled her *Carmen* performances) by inviting her to sing both operas (spaced out in the 1935 season) and *L'Italiana* as well. Correspondence exists between her and the management of Covent Garden (Beecham and Toye) laying down who should and who should not sing with her in the 1935 season, which makes very amusing reading in its *prima-donna*-ish tone of voice.

Supervia was 'of the theatre' and relished the opportunities for surprise both on the stage and off it. Her voice was a marvellously rich organ, possessing a vibrato at the top which was, in her handling of it for various effects, perfectly acceptable and gave it a special vibrant quality. Everywhere behind her performances an infectious gaiety and youthfulness come through which cannot help but charm and delight. Her early death (in childbirth) at the age of forty came as a real loss to the operatic world, for nobody since has been able to invest these coloratura mezzo roles with such panache, even supposing that there has since been such a coloratura mezzo voice.

Joan Sutherland

Joan Sutherland was born near Sydney, Australia, on 7 November 1926, and was trained in Sydney by John and Aida Dickens. She made her début there in the Australian première of Eugene Goossens's opera *Judith*, in 1950, singing the named role. In 1951 she went to London and continued her vocal studies with Clive Carey who was largely responsible for her getting into the Covent Garden company. She was first heard there as the First Lady in *Die Zauberflöte* in 1952. In that year and the following one she sang the small though much coveted part of Clothilde in *Norma* with Maria Callas, and the (offstage) Priestess in Callas's *Aida*. Joan Sutherland's first leading rolé was as a replacement Amelia in *Ballo* during the 1952–3 season at Covent Garden, and in the following year she shared Agathe in *Der Freischütz*, taking it over altogether in 1954–5. In 1955 she created Jenifer in Tippett's *Midsummer Marriage*, sang a dazzling Antonia in *Tales of Hoffmann* and excelled in several other roles without achieving the promotion that many people felt she deserved. Apart from Covent Garden, Joan Sutherland had done sterling work for the Handel Opera Society in London, for which her several different roles received abundant praise. In 1957 she sang her first Gilda in Rigoletto and proved that she was a more than usually good singer. In 1959, Covent Garden mounted the first *Lucia di Lammermoor* since 1925, and after the first night, Joan Sutherland had achieved the status of *prima donna*. Invitations followed swiftly from Vienna, Hamburg and Venice. She added further coloratura roles to her repertoire: La Sonnambula and Violetta; and her great success at the Paris Opera as Lucia was followed by Elvira in *I Puritani* at Glyndebourne. She made her début at the Met as Lucia in 1961. Joan Sutherland specialises in the partly forgotten coloratura roles and her vocal technique and beauty go from strength to strength. She is married to the musicologist and conductor, Richard Bonynge, with whom she invariably works, and has recorded leading roles in about twenty operas. In 1979 she was created D.B.E. She lives in London.

Richard Tauber

Richard Tauber was born in Linz on 16 May 1891 and named Denemy after his mother, a soubrette singer in operetta. As a boy he toured with her and began to get the theatre in his blood. When he was seven, his father Richard Anton Tauber, a theatre manager, took charge of the boy, and they moved to Wiesbaden where Tauber *père* was the director of the Opera House. But young Richard was not legally adopted, nor his name changed to Tauber, until 1922. He met musicians and singers of a different kind in Wiesbaden and decided to become a conductor. He studied at Frankfurt-am-Main but at the age of twenty switched to singing, at which he had previously shown no great talent. After study with Karl Beines in Freiburg, he was offered a four-year contract at Wiesbaden by the Director on the strength of his singing Tamino's first aria from *Die Zauberflöte*, but his father advised Richard against taking it, and he devoted the next year to additional study. His début was at Chemnitz (now Karl Marxstadt) as Tamino on 2 March 1913, and a few days later he achieved a real triumph as Max in *Der Freischütz*. This was heard by a talent scout from Dresden and Tauber was accordingly offered a five-year contract to sing there, the noblest, most advanced and glorious opera house in Europe. Von Seebach, the enlightened Director, encouraged and helped the young tenor, and Tauber profited greatly from being among the finest singers of the time. In 1922 he went to Vienna, taking with him seventy leading tenor roles, all in German. He was the first Vienna Calaf in *Turandot* in 1926, opposite Lotte Lehmann with whom his voice was well matched in this and many other operas. Tauber's early fame as a Mozart singer led Richard Strauss to cast him as Don Ottavio in the first

Richard Tauber

Maggie Teyte

opera performance at the newly constituted Salzburg Festival in 1922, and this was followed by Belmonte in *Entführung*. He returned once, in 1926, to repeat these roles.

In 1924 Tauber had become very friendly with Franz Lehár while singing in Berlin as a guest artist. Lehár composed four operettas especially for Tauber, and the fifth, *Land of Smiles*, he sang about 700 times. He thus divided his life between opera and operetta, proud to give different sections of the public what they wanted to hear. He also appeared in films and was an easily recognisable figure to everybody, in photograph or cartoon. Partly because of his operetta stigma, Tauber was not invited to Covent Garden until 1938 when he sang Tamino and Belmonte, and in 1939 when he sang Don Ottavio in a season which included Gigli, Torsten Ralf, Jussi Bjørling and Lauritz Melchior among the other tenors. Because he was a Jew he had first to leave Germany and then Austria and came to London where he composed and appeared in (or conducted) the operetta *Old Chelsea*. Because of the British firm line between opera and operetta, Tauber was excluded from both the Sadler's Wells Opera Company and the new Covent Garden Company in 1946, although he was in London for most of the time. He toured North America in 1931, 1938 and 1947, and in the latter year made his very last appearance on the opera stage, at Covent Garden on 27 September, when he was begged to sing Don Ottavio with the visiting Vienna State Opera. He went into a nursing home a few days later and never recovered.

Tauber was twice married, first to the operetta singer Carlotta Vanconti, and then to the English actress Diana Napier. His infectious good humour, his big personality and his sheer joy of living were all brave covers to certain disappointments over his career, his weak eye (the monocle) and a defective leg (the limp). Tauber was a true servant to the public because he always gave every audience what it wanted, even though he might be personally exhausted with the endless performances of 'You are my heart's delight'. But, great Mozart singer as he was, he always sang everything, no matter what it was, as though it were Mozart. His impeccable last performance of Don Ottavio showed what a perfect voice he had, how well preserved and cared for it was, and how none of its style or power had left it despite far too little use. His voice had a very individual timbre that his detractors called 'throaty' but it was warm and subject to the minutest details of shading and subtleties. He knew he was a great artist, but even so would never let anybody play a record of his after one of Caruso's. 'Caruso', he said, 'is still the King of Tenors.'

Maggie Teyte

Maggie Teyte was born Tate in Wolverhampton on 17 April 1888 (the day before Frida Leider). She first studied voice at the Royal College of Music, and from 1905 in Paris with Jean de Reszke. From this time she seemed to be more French than English, concentrating upon the *chanson* and involving herself in French musical life. Her operatic début was at Monte Carlo as Zerlina in *Don Giovanni* in 1907, and in the following year she went to the Opéra-Comique in Paris where she created the part of Glycère in Hillemacher's opera *Circe*. In 1908, at Debussy's special request, and after coaching from him, Maggie Teyte took over the role of Mélisande and remained at the Opéra-Comique until 1910. She was to be heard in Paris in these years, giving recitals of *chansons* with Debussy at the piano. She went to London in 1910 for Beecham's winter season at Covent Garden, where she sang Mélisande and Marguerite in *Faust*. Between 1911 and 1914 Maggie Teyte was with the Chicago Opera and in 1914 she sang Cherubino at Covent Garden. After the First World War she joined the British National Opera Company in their 1922–3 season at Covent Garden, singing a glorious Butterfly, a thoroughly boyish and delightful Hänsel and her famous Cherubino. She also created the part of the Princess in the première of Gustav Holst's one-act opera *The Perfect Fool*. In 1930 she returned to sing Butterfly and Mélisande but was not heard there again until the Coronation Season of 1937. A new production of Gluck's *Orpheus* with the De Basil Ballet somewhat misfired, but Maggie Teyte's singing of Eurydice was never in doubt. Her last appearances at the Royal Opera were as Hänsel and Butterfly later that year. During the Second World War Mme Teyte sang to entertain the troops and gave an especially memorable concert at the National Gallery on French Independence Day 1944. In 1946 she gave a long and successful concert tour in North America and sang Mélisande at the New York City Centre in 1948. In 1951 she joined Kirsten Flagstad (*q.v.*) at the Mermaid Theatre in London for the special production of *Dido and Aeneas* in the Festival of Britain year, when she sang

Belinda. This was her last operatic appearance, although she again undertook concert tours in North America and in Britain as late as 1954.

Owing to her long stay in France, Mme Teyte was able to invest her French roles with great authority, and her singing of Mélisande brought Debussy's intentions forward almost half a century. Her voice was of very great lyrical, limpid beauty and her technique and artistry were supreme. The greatest tribute that could be paid her, from another singer and another Mélisande, came from Dora Labbette who said: 'Among us British sopranos, and I include mezzo-sopranos, was one who could do it all. Maggie Teyte was the greatest of all of us.' Created D.B.E. in 1968, she died on 26 May 1976.

Richard Tucker

Richard Tucker, tenor, was born Reuben Ticker (Ticher) in Brooklyn on 20 August 1913. At the age of six he sang in the choir of a New York Synagogue, but he did not pursue his career as a professional singer until somewhat later. In his late twenties he studied with the celebrated American *Heldentenor* and teacher, Paul Althouse, and gave his concert début in New York at the age of thirty-one. Richard Tucker then joined a touring company called the Salmaggi Opera, and first sang at the Met in 1945, as Enzo Grimaldo in Ponchielli's *La Gioconda*. This began his highly successful career there, accelerated by his 1949 radio performance of Radamès in *Aida* conducted by Toscanini. This was later recorded. Richard Tucker was the Met's leading tenor in the Italian and French repertoire (as well as Alfred in *Die Fledermaus* and Lenski in *Eugen Onegin*) for more than twenty-five years. In 1947 he sang in *La Gioconda* at the Verona Arena opposite Maria Callas (who was making her Italian début) and afterwards went to La Scala as a guest tenor, as well as taking up engagements at San Francisco, Los Angeles and Chicago. His tours included appearances at Covent Garden in 1958 as Cavaradossi in *Tosca*, at Vienna, and in Israel and South America, as well as throughout North America. He died suddenly in New York on 8 January 1975 of a heart attack. His apparently tireless and always powerful tenor voice had no rival for stamina in the Italian repertoire, save perhaps from Mario del Monaco.

Richard Tucker as Rodolfo in La Bohème

Ludwig Weber

Ludwig Weber was born on 29 July 1899 in Vienna. At first intended to be a schoolmaster, he trained at the Vienna School of Art under the great scenic designer, Alfred Roller. His voice made itself apparent in the Vienna Oratorio Society to which he belonged, and so he had it properly trained by Alfred Boruttau and devoted himself to music. He made his début with the Vienna Volksoper in 1920, remaining there for five years singing small parts until, in 1925, he became principal bass at the Barmen–Elberfeld Opera (now Wuppertal). He moved to Düsseldorf in 1927, and in 1930 was a guest artist at the Théâtre des Champs-Elysées for a season of Wagner operas under the direction of the Bayreuth conductor, Franz von Hoesslin. Weber was at Cologne between 1930 and 1933 and then joined the Munich ensemble, remaining a member there until 1945. He first appeared at Covent Garden as Pogner, Gurnemanz, Hunding and Hagen in the 1936 season; he added Daland in 1937 and Osmin and Rocco in 1938. In 1939 he was heard at Salzburg as the Commendatore on 9 August, but appeared there only once more, as Sarastro, in 1941, until after the war. In 1945 he received the call he had been waiting for, to come home to Vienna, and at last made his début on the Ring and among the ruins. From 1945 he visited Salzburg (Osmin, the Commendatore, Doctor Bartolo and St Just in the première of von Einem's *Dantons Tod*). He went to London with the Vienna State

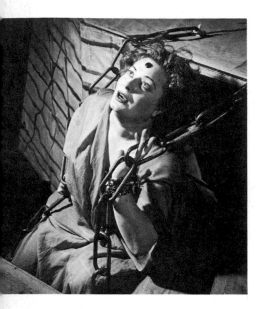

Ljuba Welitsch as Salome

Opera in 1947 and in the 1949–50 *Ring* cycles there he sang Hunding and Hagen. Weber was now at the peak of his career and in 1951 was called to Bayreuth for the reopening where he sang Fasolt, Hagen and Gurnemanz. He sang there in nearly every season for the next ten years. He was last heard in London with the Vienna State Opera during their second post-war visit, at the Royal Festival Hall, when he sang the Commendatore. He sang at the Theater Cólon in Buenos Aires but never in the United States.

Weber was possibly the best Gurnemanz, Hunding and Hagen of this century, and the number of times he sang these roles ensured a deep understanding and a maturer interpretation of them than any other bass was able to accomplish. His Rocco, Pogner and Daland were other fine examples of his great art. His true bass voice was of exceptional beauty even when it was used for such ugly characters as Hunding and Hagen. His Gurnemanz exploited all his reserves of subtlety and *mezza voce* singing and his diction was perfect. Ludwig Weber was a professor at the Salzburg Mozarteum from 1961 for ten years and he died in Vienna on 9 December 1974.

Ljuba Welitsch

Ljuba Welitsch was born Velichkova at Borisovo, Bulgaria, on 10 July 1913. She studied singing at the Conservatoire in Sofia, then in Vienna with Theo Lierhammer. Her début was at Sofia in 1936, and she then went to Graz for four years. Between 1940 and 1943 she sang at Hamburg and appeared as a guest soprano at the Berlin State Opera and at Dresden. In 1943 she became a member of the Munich ensemble until she was called to Vienna in 1945. As a guest in Vienna in 1944 she sang Salome during the week to celebrate Richard Strauss's eightieth birthday and was described by him as 'the ideal interpreter'. She sang this role – and Donna Anna – with the Vienna State Opera at Covent Garden in 1947 and also appeared with Jay Pomeroy's Opera Company at the Cambridge Theatre. Her performance in London as the soprano soloist (with Elisabeth Hoengen, Julius Patzak and Norman Walker) of Beethoven's Choral Symphony under Furtwängler in 1947 will always be remembered by those who heard it for Welitsch's fiery and inspired singing, in a very operatic manner. Between 1947 and 1953 Welitsch appeared at Covent Garden eleven times as Salome, but six of these performances were in the notorious Brook–Dali production. Otherwise she sang Aida, Musetta, Tosca and Lisa (*Queen of Spades*). At the Edinburgh Festival of 1948 she was a passionate Amelia in *Un Ballo in Maschera*. In that year she first appeared at the Metropolitan Opera, but it was on 4 February 1949 that she became a star with her Salome. A year later on 3 February 1950 she delighted Met audiences as Donna Anna; and at a gala evening in honour of Edward Johnson's retirement as general manager, in April 1950, she sang a vivid and larger-than-life Tosca. Since 1955 Mme Welitsch has made films and appeared in operetta, but made a sudden return to the Met to act the part of the eccentric Countess in Donizetti's *La Fille du Régiment* with Joan Sutherland. She was immensely popular in this comic character, to which she applied her whole art.

Ljuba Welitsch always created a sensation whenever she appeared because she was far larger than life, and has bright red hair. She was electrifying both on and off the stage, but added to this enormous dramatic advantage was the voice, a sensual instrument, very pure and girlish in timbre, yet with sufficient power (and retention of beauty) to ride the huge orchestra of *Salome*. Even in her last appearances at Covent Garden in 1953, when the voice had sadly diminished in power, every word was heard, every note was truly and accurately placed. She is a real *prima donna*, one of the last, with her aura of magnificence, her dominating personality, her very size, her laugh, and her very big heart.

VIII Bravo! Bravo! Arcibravo!

The emotional experience of an opera differs from the response to a play, a ballet or a concert. A spontaneous cry of joy from the audience after a well-sung aria or duet as a punctuation to the performance is a continuous stamp of approval and as such it is welcomed by the singers. But have we not heard tyros being hissed to silence for daring to applaud after the first movement of a symphony?

Any performance is, in a sense, an attempt by artists to win over the audience *en masse* to their side by their efforts, although this is not to say that the audience is playing hard to get every time. Among each audience there will be (for a tried and tested opera) a handful of people who have never heard the work before. Others will not have the least idea what it is about and will not possess sufficient interest to find out. Others will have slight knowledge of the opera from records or the radio, and a few (musicians and students most likely, probably at the extreme ends of the gallery, where it meets the proscenium wall in older opera houses) will have brought the score along and be prepared to take another approach by hearing and reading, though seldom looking at the spectacle.

Then there are the 'experts', otherwise known as 'opera buffs' who are chalking up ten, twenty or more performances of this very opera, and whose interest in it may not seem altogether normal. Either they are going as fans of a particular singer, or as members of an opera club, or they are cranks whose every evening is spent in the opera house.

The opera has always attracted its special devotees, either eccentrics or intelligent people with a real taste for the art who are taking it perfectly seriously in an effort to widen their own perceptions. In the nineteenth century in Paris, there was a large coterie of young men about town who were regular frequenters of the Opéra. They were so indispensable to the economy of the house that composers were obliged to bear them in mind when preparing new works for Paris. It was, however, a curiosity that has not so far been repeated,

Franco Zeffirelli, Tito Gobbi, Maria Callas and Renato Cioni taking a curtain call after Act II of Tosca *in 1964*

Previous page: Maria Callas receiving a bouquet from one of the wigged footmen on the stage of Covent Garden

184

for the young men went there solely to pay court to the ballet girls. Their interest in the opera itself was negligible, but without them it is doubtful whether Wagner would ever have needed to compose the Venusberg ballet in *Tannhäuser*, or Rossini the ballet music for *Guillaume Tell*.

In the nineteenth century the Opera (with a capital 'O') was a grand social affair, and so it remained until 1914 in Europe, staggering along not so comfortably between the two world wars until it became state-aided, though with a great deal of difference in the amount of aid according to the state concerned. The pictures on pages 186 and 187 show different types of audiences and present an interesting contrast. One shows the special circumstances created by the English 'Prom' transferred from the Royal Albert Hall. But as an opera audience they are not yet representative. In direct contrast, the other picture shows the Royal Opera House decked out for the 1953 Coronation Gala Performance, again not characteristic of its appearance.

Yet this is a more suitable and recognisable surrounding to the top-hatted gentlemen and heavily bejewelled ladies who are shown in the Paris Opéra picture. They are merely an extension in dress and behaviour of those earlier opera patrons who went there merely to talk, play cards, and make love in their boxes between the acts. But when the castrati performed their heavily ornamented arias, the audience paid heed.

Opera bravos still exist today, in different guise. They are young (and not so young) men who, beautifully dressed, make their entrance to the opera house in trousers perhaps a little too tight. They nod to the attendants, leave their cloaks and canes, and after subtle adjustments in a looking-glass, walk carefully through the throng to mid-way up the staircase where they pause, thoughtfully, and survey the scene. Needless to say, they too can be surveyed in this position by those below and above. Perhaps a discreet wave to somebody, real or pretended, the flash of a smile and then on and up to the bar. Their special corner is already populated, and then they get going. Voices are raised so as to

Below left: A Dandy recovering from a shock in a side-box during the opera in the nineteenth century

Below: A foyer of the Paris Opéra in 1908, during an interval. Since the gentlemen were in a public place, equivalent to being in the street, they kept on their hats until they re-entered their boxes in the opera house

attract bystanders with their obviously knowledgeable conversation in which singers' first names, and pet names of course, are bandied about, together with their latest doings. What is going to happen once the curtain has gone up seems already to be known to these *cognoscenti*, and during the intervals their prescience is borne out. Once the performance has begun these astute gentlemen, scattered among the expensive seats, proceed to lead the rest of the audience with applause and vociferous shouts in Italian, taking care to use the right endings to '*Brav-*', depending upon whether it is feminine or masculine, singular or plural. Afterwards they collect a small party and go to the restaurant most favoured by singers that season – they know where to go. They might stoop to asking for an autograph and congratulating a singer with apparent insight into the overcoming of a technical difficulty in the performance, but will under no circumstances congregate among the hoi-polloi at the stage door.

The desperate seeking and fulfilment of a satisfying outlet by highly emotional people can often be achieved at an opera performance. If this seems an exaggerated statement it is, after all, a higher-minded and slightly less acute state of excitement than that which the very young suffer at their pop concerts, where they can be driven into a state of hysteria until they have to be carried out. The difference lies in a delicately balanced and varied musical entertainment contrasted with a monotony and insistence of sound so great in volume and repetition that it assaults and overcomes.

It is in the upper reaches of the opera house that the appreciation and devotion to singers and the opera are generally found to be most rational and sincere. Here the audience is no less knowledgeable than elsewhere, but all their effort is subjected towards enjoyment of the performance, and drinking it in objectively. When Gigli first sang in London he was criticised for playing to the gallery, but he knew what he was doing and secured their valuable support, although at the expense of the rejected stall-holders.

There was once a man – perhaps he is still alive – who used to frequent a certain opera house gallery. He always had the same seat, though was never seen in the queue to get it, and was guaranteed to put in three nights a week there, in the centre of the front row, and always on first nights. This went on for years. But the most extraordinary – and unhappy – thing about him was that he hardly ever spoke to anybody during the intervals, never smiled, and, when the opera was over, left his seat immediately, barging past people's knees so as to get out as quickly as possible and without applauding. How much he took in or enjoyed or learnt from it is impossible to judge because he gave no reaction at any time. It was almost as if he was on duty there for some secret purpose divorced from the performance. But he could not stand any interruptions round him and was rude to anybody who spoke or whispered.

Fortunately such people are few and far between, for an audience should be a cheerful and sociable body who can enjoy and profit from discussion during intervals, even with strangers.

There is another member of an audience who has his circle of admirers on first nights: the professional critic. He is usually a somewhat evasive creature, running far from enquiring members of the audience who want to get an opinion from the horse's mouth so that they can astonish their friends. The critic is a journalist who normally leaves the opera house for the nearest bar during the interval, where he may even meet colleagues from other papers and compare notes. If he finds the performance tedious, or has another notice to write elsewhere (as sometimes happens) he must be careful to check up afterwards that nothing of great importance happened while he was absent, in case his review on the following day betrays his ignorance.

Stalls area at Covent Garden Opera House with seats removed for the 'Opera Proms'. The conductor is about to arrive at his desk (right-hand corner)

Because the opera is such an expensive undertaking, the best way for the management to ensure paid attendance is by subscription. On special nights there may be three times as many people as the house can hold, all trying to get in. Then a black market in tickets will develop. But the subscribers will be safe. Festival performances of opera (which began at Bayreuth in 1876) have now proliferated beyond the capacity of managements to provide orchestras and singers to the expected standards.

Bayreuth Festival audiences have changed dramatically even since the Festspielhaus reopened in 1951. In that season elderly Prussians with duelling scars and fans (for it was rather warm) seemed to be relics from the end of the last century. Much of the tradition and procedure from the first festival there still obtains. Hundreds of local inhabitants line the route from the roundabout at the bottom of *der Hügel* all the way to the top on the day of the *Generalprobe* (reserved for Bayreuthers) and thereafter on performance afternoons, for time of start is as early as 4 p.m. Car-loads of smart spectators drive past the crowds and each is commented on before it is decanted outside the main entrance (if very important) or round at the back. This procedure varies not at all from the year 1936 when Hitler 'took over' Bayreuth and attended the Festival. Before each act, three brass players appear on a balcony above the crowd and play a special fanfare which Wagner composed with the music of the forthcoming act in mind.

A unique opera festival takes place every summer at Glyndebourne in Sussex, in a fold of the South Downs. It began in 1934 when Mr John Christie, formerly a chemistry master at Eton and always an amateur of the opera (in the Victorian sense), built a small opera house to accommodate an audience of 300 adjoining his family seat near Lewes. He obtained the collaboration of Carl Ebert from Berlin as producer and Fritz Busch from Dresden as conductor, and

Below: The Royal Opera House Covent Garden on the occasion of the Coronation Gala performance in the presence of HM the Queen and members of the Royal Family on 8 June 1953. Oliver Messel designed the decorations

their casts for *Figaro* and *Così fan Tutte* were drawn from among the best singers to be found in Europe. The total integration and love which was bestowed on everybody working there ensured a standard of ensemble and of production not witnessed in England in living memory, perhaps never before. Glyndebourne prospered ('evening dress is recommended'), and Industry underwrites any deficit, not the taxpayer.

Nowadays, more than ever before, Industry is helping to finance the opera. Patronage has passed from princes to rich men like Sir Joseph Beecham, and his son, Sir Thomas, to committees and arts councils recommending and never getting the kind of subsidy required to keep the art alive, let alone in a flourishing, experimental and developing manner. Government subsidies merely hint at true requirements, and with rising costs, strikes and deterioration in the very fabric of the buildings, the perfect world of Opera is unable to remain aloof from the imperfect world outside. While industrial support is a fine thing, it sometimes means that a block of seats which an oil company, a bank or a chainstore has bought in advance for the whole season may be empty, while the general public are queueing outside and cannot get in. It also means that employees of these firms will be offered opera seats at a very reduced rate, even for nothing, and may thus be introduced to a new experience.

Probably the most important section of an audience is the young people who have never before heard the opera which is being sung. Their future impressions of it will be judged by *their* personal première. They are the people to impress, to delight, to stamp with the memory of a vivid and acceptable interpretation, so that in years to come, one hopes, they will recall with delight the night when they heard X or Y singing. 'Those were the days, there's nobody nowadays who can touch them.' But that's what older people have a habit of saying.

So, given this mixed assembly in the front of the house, all sitting facing the same direction, most of them agog, and some very excited, what are they to expect for what they have given? Nowadays what it has cost them to participate in the ritual is, in Western cities, a great deal. And a ritual it most certainly is. Evening dress is no longer compulsory, except on state occasions, and it is interesting to note that Italian audiences are, in the main, the smartest; American the most self-conscious; British the scruffiest and least presentable; German and Austrian the most conscious of its being an occasion and therefore deserving reverence; and the French – nonchalant.

Nobody who has paid for his seat is likely to consider very seriously that he has entirely overlooked the subsidy which has enabled him to gain admittance for less than what it is all costing the management. Nor will he have thought about the amount of effort and patience which has gone into the production. All this will be taken for granted since he has come to get what he considers to be his money's worth in one way or another. Admittedly some of the audience only come to pass the evening in a comfortable chair with pleasant thoughts of the bar during the next interval to carry them through those dull parts; others like to sleep because the tickets were only passed on by some friends who had to fly to Greece; others enjoy the spectacle, the rest of the audience and the enjoyment of the ritual. But there is more to being a member of the audience than this.

If some kind of enthusiasm is generated on the stage, it is bound to be felt by the audience, who must respond accordingly. This response bounces back into pit and on to the stage, to and fro, until every person there is caught up by the excitement and welded together as a single unity. When this happens there is no longer audience and artists, the gap between stage and auditorium has been firmly bridged, and the result will be a staggering performance.

188

Auditorium of the Metropolitan Opera House, New York, opening night, November 1946

Of course no audience is going to be martialled – consciously – or made to feel that it is under any obligation, having paid to come in and sit down. But there are certain members of an audience in some opera houses called the 'claque'. They are paid by one or more of the singers to support him or her throughout the performance with (hopefully) such a weight of *bravos* that the rest of the audience is convinced that the object of attention is perhaps better than they had realised. The claque is to be found mainly in Italian opera houses, and at the Vienna Opera where it goes back a long way in the history of the house.

A claque is something of a curiosity in a country where freedom of choice, thought and action is said to pertain, for it can be rather evil in seeking to dominate an audience by sheer brute force. On the other hand, claques and anti-claques can produce turmoil and funny scenes when they get going. But that is not at all what going to the opera is meant to be about. Few people wish to have their evening disturbed by the semblance of a riot, and far prefer the usurpers of their peace and quiet to fight it out at the stage door.

The performance should end with applause from the heart, a large bouquet for the *prima donna*, a red rose to the tenor, repeated calls for the soloists, one at a time, then the whole cast again and again with the conductor (dishevelled but happy). Finally the curtain comes down to stay, the audience slowly leave, and there is now no more than a glimmer in the empty auditorium where crumpled programmes and empty chocolate boxes litter the huge silence.

189

Further Reading List

Dent, Edward J. *Opera*. Harmondsworth: Penguin Books, 1940.

Grove, George *Dictionary of Music and Musicians*, 6th edition, London: Macmillan, and New York: St. Martin's Press, 1982.

Hammelmann, Richard, and Ewald Osers *The Correspondence between Richard Strauss and Hugo von Hofmannsthal*, London: Collins, 1961.

Hartnoll, Phyllis (ed.) *Oxford Companion to the Theatre*. London: Oxford University Press, 1957.

Jacobs, Arthur (ed.) *British Music Yearbooks*. London and New York: Bowker, 1973–82.

Kaut, Josef *Festspiele in Salzburg*. Munich, 1970.

Kobbé's Complete Opera Book, 9th edition, edited and revised by the Earl of Harewood. London: Putnam, 1976.

Kutsch, Karl Josef, and Leo Riemens (eds.) *A concise biographical dictionary of singers*. Philadelphia, 1969.

Rosenthal, Harold *Two Centuries of Opera at Covent Garden*. London and New York: Putnam, 1958.

Scholes, Percy A. (ed.) *Oxford Companion to Music*. 10th edition, London, Oxford University Press, 1980.

Wechsberg, Joseph *Looking for a Bluebird*. London: Michael Joseph, 1946.

Acknowledgements

The publisher would like to thank the following for permission to reproduce photographs in this book:

Black and white
The author: 15, 42, 94; BBC: 88–89; Bayreuth Opera: 74tl, 74c, 74b; Beth Bergman: 108, 143; Zoe Dominic: 117, 153, 166; Zoe Dominic Photography/Catherine Ashmore 174; Glyndebourne Opera, photographs by Guy Gravett: 102, 103, 126, 152; Italian State Tourist Office: 22; Keystone Press Agency: 35; London Coliseum, photographs by John Garner: 64, 65; Mander and Mitchenson Theatre Collection: 6–7, 29, 36t, 39, 40, 47, 63t, 67, 92, 164b, 184b, 188; Mansell Collection: 8, 16r, 20, 21, 25, 33, 50, 156, 161, 185b, endpapers; Robin May Collection: 184–5; Mermaid Theatre: 117; lennart Af Petersens: 68b; Popperphoto: 12, 13, 161, 49, 661, 75, 86, 155, 157, 162, 164–5, 166, 166tr, 168, 172r, 179b; RCA Records: 170l; Stuart Robinson: 135; Houston Rogers: 2–3, 10, 11, 31, 44, 54, 57, 67r, 77t, 78, 79, 83, 84, 93, 97t, 101, 110t, 110b, 112, 127, 128, 132, 136, 137, 138–9, 142, 146l, 154, 160, 177, 183; Harold Rosenthal: 173, 180; Royal Opera House Covent Garden Archives: 30, 37, 59t, 68t, 110tl, 111b, 113, 118t, 118b, 120, 121, 129, 133t, 134, 147, 163, 170, 172l, 175, 176, 179t, 181, 186–7b; Royal Opera House Covent Garden Press Office: 186t; Donald Southern: 18, 56, 77bl, 77br, 82, 99, 100t, 107, 130, 141r, 146r, 158; Sport and General: 48: Reg Wilson: 59t, 62, 63b, 73t, 73b, 81, 95, 114, 115, 133b, 145; Roger Wood: 47b, 90t, 90b, 100b, 116, 140, 159, 182.

Colour
The author, photographs by Paul Forrester: 71; Beth Bergman: 160; Zoe Dominic: 124; Giraudon: 18–19; Erich Lessing/Magnum: 54; Mansell Collection: 17t, 17b; Reg Wilson: 105t, 105b; ZEFA: 72b, 106t, 106b, 123, 157t, 157b, 158t, 158b, 158–9; ZEFA-Snark: 20t, 20b, 53t, 53b, 72t.

Index

This Index is arranged in two sections:
I People II Operas
The following abbreviations are used in Section I:

Aus. = Austrian
Br. = British
Bulg. = Bulgarian
Can. = Canadian
Cz. = Czech
Dan. = Danish
Eng. = English
Fr. = French
Grk. = Greek
Ger. = German
Hung. = Hungarian
It. = Italian
Nor. = Norwegian
Pol. = Polish
Russ. = Russian
Span. = Spanish
Swed. = Swedish
US. = Citizen of USA
Yug. = Yugoslav

bar. = baritone
bs-bar. = bass baritone
comp. = composer
con. = contralto
cond. = conductor
des. = designer
imp. = impresario
lib. = librettist
mgr. = manager
prod. = producer
sop. = soprano
ten. = tenor
trans. = translator

Figures in italics refer to illustrations.

People

191

192